The Concept of Tradition in Ballad Research

A Symposium

D0746038

ODENSE UNIVERSITY PRESS

The publication of this volume was made possible by a grant from
Odense University on the recommendation of professor Julia McGrew
and arkivar Jens Henrik Koudal

Proceedings of the Ninth International Symposium
organized by the
Centre for the Study of Vernacular Literature
in the Middle Ages
Held at Odense University
on 19-20 November, 1984

Edited by
Rita Pedersen
Flemming G. Andersen

© 1985 by Odense University Press
ISBN: 87 7492 562 8

Printed by Special-Trykkeriet Viborg a-s
Cover design by Sonia Brandes
Paper cutting: "Til sagn og sange og eventyr
jeg lytted, da jeg var lille"

Contents

Preface

The Symposium on The Concept of Tradition in Ballad Research was held at Odense University on 19-20 November, 1984. The book as here presented contains the papers in the order in which they were read, together with the opponents' speeches and summaries of the ensuing discussions.

The Symposium was the ninth of its kind, organized by the *Centre for the Study of Vernacular Literature in the Middle Ages*. We wish to express our sincere gratitude to Odense University, The Danish Research Council for the Humanities and Ingeniør N. M. Knudsens Fond for the generous help and support that made possible the arrangement of the Symposium and the publication of the proceedings.

The Editors

Session 1

Tradition: Objectivations or Social Behaviour?

Written paper
BY REIMUND KVIDELAND

Tradition is a key word in folklore research and used in many different meanings.

To me tradition is a symbolic process and in accordance with this concept I have for the last ten years argued for a study of *singing activities*,1) a term I prefer to performance. I find the latter too closely related to the artistic aspect of folklore, an aspect underlined by Dan Ben-Amos in his definition of folklore as artistic communication in small groups,2) and by H. Glassie in his comments upon the definition of Ben-Amos.3)

I do not deny the importance of the artistic aspect, but I would emphasize folklore as a structured rather than an artistic communication.

It is important to underline the communicative and interactionistic aspect of tradition. Singing should be seen not only from the artistic and aesthetic aspect but also, and primarily, as a musical communication.

On many occasions I have pointed to Jon-Roar Bjørkvold's study of children's spontaneous singing, our musical mother tongue,4) as an example of how fruitful this aspect can be. Another example is

1. Reimund Kvideland, "Folk Ballad and Folk Song", Studia Fennica 27 (1983), 177-83.
2. Dan Ben-Amos, "Toward a Definition of Folklore in Context", Journal of American Folklore, 84 (1971), 3-15.
3. Henry Glassie, "The Moral Lore of Folklore", Folklore Forum, 16:2 (1983), p. 129f.
4. Jon-Roar Bjørkvold, "Den spontane barnesangen - vårt musikalske morsmål". Diss. Oslo, 1980. 2 Vols.

the study by Pàivikki Suojanen, who has demonstrated very clearly
how a musical language is used by a religious group.5)

To study tradition as socio-cultural behaviour or activity means
to attach importance to *why* people sing as well as what, when,
where, and how people sing. The point of departure should be the
singing and not the texts.

It is not the scope of this paper to develop all the problems
raised by this approach, I will only point out some of the most
important.

First, should we limit our scope to certain parts of singing
activities? In an earlier paper I have proposed that our field of
research should include all singing activities except stage performances by professional singers.6) But probably even this activity
should be considered by folklorists, because there is a constant and
considerable influence by stage performances on popular singing
activitites. This problem of limitations is a serious one from a
theoretical point of view.

Secondly this approach demands that we look at the phenomenon from several angles and that we use a variety of methods of
analysis. I see the following as the most important: A combined
text and context analysis in which the ethnolinguistic method must
play an important role.

One result should be an understanding of the world view of
individual singers and groups of singers.

The emotions created by singing must be examined from a
musical-psychological point of wiew, and this should include an
analysis of needs and functions.

From a musical-sociological point of view, the group dynamics,
the relations between the group members, and the roles actualised
through singing must be considered. Another aspect is the role of

5. Päivikki Suojanen, "Den religiösa mötessångens gruppdynamik.
   En etnomusikologisk undersökning av religiös mötessång",
   Sumlen 1981, 94–108.
6. R. Kvideland, "Folkeleg songtradisjon som brukspoesi", in Elin
   Prøysen, Folkelige viser. Norsk folkeminnelags skrifter 109,
   Oslo, 1973, p. 12. R. Kvideland, "Synspunkter på vise-forskinga i
   dag", Sumlen 1976, p. 198. Cf. J.M. Rahmelow, "Das Volkslied
   als publizistisches Medium und historische Quelle", Jahrbuch für
   Volksliedforschung, 14 (1969), p. 13.

the entrepreneurs. It is important to investigate who provides the songs and the music, who controls the subject matter of songs. Producers, distributors and the mass media are important factors. In the following I will discuss some of the consequences of this approach for our concept of tradition.

The most common meaning given to the term *tradition* is a set of objectivations of popular culture. *Tradition* is there used more or less synonymously with *folklore*. This is the case in the Scandinavian languages (which lack an exact equivalant to folklore), in German, Italian etc.

On the other hand American folklorists have in the recent years been more cautious or reluctant in using the term tradition, preferring folklore instead.

Secondly tradition means a form of communication or a process. This includes folklore as 'artistic communication in small groups' and at the same time it underlines the aspect of time. Tradition as such is passed on from one generation to another. This means that modern folklore and innovations may or may not become tradition, depending on the ability and willingness of the users to pass them on to a new generation and the latter's interest in accepting them. In this sense tradition dictates the limits of folklore research in a way which is open to question.

A third meaning includes tradition as a quality, sometimes with negative but usually with positive connotations, based on qualities such as age and naturality.

The first concept, that of tradition as a set of objectivations dominates both scholarly and lay thought.

The basic attitudes that determined and dominated this concept of tradition are irrationality, orality, rurality, anonymity, continuity, communality and universality.

It is difficult to rule out any of these attributes, but all of them are problematic and none of them should be used literally. Each of them could be worth a paper or a seminar, so I will make some short comments on some of them.

The concept of orality has often been challenged and modified, many arguments are put forward in the highly recommended special issue of *Narodna umjetnost: Folklore and oral communication* edited by Maja Bošković-Stulli.7)

7.   M. Bošković-Stulli, ed., <u>Folklore and Oral Communication.</u> Folk-

The concepts of rurality and continuity have been modified, and Ben-Amos, in an elucidating essay, recently pointed out that anonymity hardly solves the enigma of origin. "By default rather than merit, anonymity became an earmark of folklore."8)

Communality has become a central concept of tradition, but raises many questions and is hard to define in an operative sense.

The crucial point is that these attributes have been linked to the concept of tradition as a set of objectivations and in this combination they have generated other attributes. Since tradition in itself presupposes objectivations of a certain age, it is easy to understand that age became a criterium of quality.

One consequence of this line of thought was the concept that the ballad had to be defined as a medieval category. Even the classification of the ballad corpus is based on the concept "Middle Ages".

The two new Scandinavian ballad editions, *Norske mellomalder-balladar* and *Sveriges Medeltida Ballader*, are based on this concept.

The editors of the Swedish edition state that "Ballads unmistakably later than about 1520, and various kinds of pastiche, are excluded."9) A logical consequence of this view is that "all variants recorded before 1810 are printed".10) I admire the scholarly work in this edition, but I question its ideological basis, as I question the concept of tradition, old, and new as interpretive terms rather than descriptive terms.

This concept of tradition as objectivations is based on methodological essentialism or the naturalistic paradigm. Folklorists have treated tradition as if it is analoguous to natural objets. The history of the ballad is seen as an analogue to the history of the oak tree or the wild horses in Europe.

Richard Handler and Jocelyn Linnekin have recently pointed out that the "naturalistic paradigm has dominated Western social

lore und mündliche Kommunikation (Zagreb, 1981), Narodna umjetnost. Special Issue.
8. D. Ben-Amos, "The Idea of Folklore: An Essay", in I. Ben-Ami and J. Dan, eds., Studies in Aggadah and Jewish Folklore. Folklore Research Center Studies 7. Jerusalem, 1983, p. 12.
9. Sveriges Medeltida Ballader, I, (Stockholm, 1983), p. 493.
10. Ibid., p. 494.

thought since the time of Edmund Burke, who was the first modern theorist of tradition."11)

They have also pointed to the important fact that the past is always constructed in the present (p. 286). This means that continuity is constructed and thereby includes an element of discontinuity. "To refer to the past, to take account of or interpret it, implies that one is located in the present, that one is distanced or apart from the object reconstructed. In sum, the relationship of prior to present representations is symbolically mediated, not naturally given; it encompasses both continuity and discontinuity. Thus we can no longer speak of tradition in terms of the approximate identity of some objective thing that changes while remaining the same."12)

If we admit this, and it is difficult not to do so, we should be willing to revise some of our concepts. It is, for example, difficult to maintain the idea of the medieval ballad constructed on material from the 18th and 19th centuries on such a basis.

And it wil be most difficult to argue that some traditions are more genuine than others because the whole question of genuineness becomes inappropriate.

In an earlier paper first given at the Nordic conference of folklore and folklife studies (1981) I showed how this concept of objectivations is based on methodological essentialism.13) Through the essentialistic thinking those attributes which are only descriptive or interpretive have acquired a normative status,14) and the objectivations have been limited to a fixed set.

Instead of understanding tradition as objectivations or natural objects, we should understand it as a symbolic process. There is a tendency to use the term process as a slogan, as a kind of a magical key that explains everything. It has been used to denote that objectivations migrate as autonomous phenomena, that tradition is passed from one person or generation to another, that tradition is always changing or growing like an organism. This is unfortunate. The term process should be reserved for the concept

11. Richard Handler and Jocelyn Linnekin, "Tradition, Genuine or Spurious", Journal of American Folklore, 97 (1984), p. 286.
12. Ibid., p. 287.
13. R. Kvideland, as note 1.
14. Cf. Ben-Amos, as note 8, p. 16.

of tradition as a store or reservoir of culturally accepted knowledge that grows and changes along with the process of enculturation. Every time it is used, it is recreated in accordance with the given situation. It includes both the message and the form of interaction. It can be presented as fixed form, as references or conversation. This concept excludes the concept of tradition as a set of objectivations. But it does not exclude the study of texts. It only demands that a context should be included.

There is a clear trend in general folklore research to move from a study of objectivations to a study of social behaviour.15) Space does not allow me to examine this in detail, I will only mention two examples.

In folk narrative research the study of fixed genres is slowly losing its dominating position. While it took many years before Otto Brinkmann's pioneer work, *Das Erzählen in einer Dorfgemeinschaft*,16) was followed by similar works, quite a few performance studies have appeared during the last decade. *Alltägliches Erzählen* and every day speech constitute the basic material in a promising list of works in which interaction rather than the text is the main focus of interest. The study of folk belief, exemplified by the study of folk medicine shows a similar tendency. The emphasis is not only on the objectivations such as magical remedies but also on healing as a socio-cultural drama, and on the concepts of health and illness.

As long as we understand tradition as objectivations these phenomena - and singing activities - must be regarded as peripheral, understood as a process, they become central.

University of Bergen

15. Cf. Arthur Simon, "Probleme, Methoden und Ziele der Ethno-musikologie", Jahrbuch für musikalische Volks- und Völkerkunde, 9 (1978), 8-52.
16. Otto Brinkmann, Das Erzählen in einer Dorfgemeinshaft. (Münster in Westfalen, 1933).

Opposition by *Kirsten Sass Bak*

It has been no secret to the organizers, I think, that Reimund Kvideland's views on these matters and mine were probably not very far from each other. This is true – so my first point will in fact be to thank Reimund Kvideland for bringing up a number of highly relevant problems in this discussion, for stressing general and fundamental theoretical aspects of the concept of 'tradition', and for – once again – making a set of valuable references to literature that is up to the day.

One might say that the various points in Reimund Kvideland's paper form a whole in which the very concept of 'tradition' is central, but where the *description of the object* (what we ought to study), and a basic view on *ways and means* in research are equally important. (I shall leave it to others, though, to label those views in relation to current *paradigms* in the the study of folklore.)

My comments in this paper will concern only a few of the problems introduced by Reimund Kvideland. I hope and trust that others will take up other parts of it – and after reading the papers from the various contributors, I feel certain that some of them will be taken up!

I have chosen to touch upon some problems which I find particularly important to keep discussing. As to whether I agree with Reimund Kvideland's opinions – or how far we do agree – this will be implied, I think; anyway this is not the important thing. But I do think it is important that we do not lose sight of the fundamental and general theoretical problems, even among the new and exciting special studies that we are looking forward to meet on this occasion.

First a point that seems to me a pseudo–problem. Reimund Kvideland refers to the question – well-known to scholars of folklore – of *limitations within the field of objects of research*. Should we restrict ourselves to investigate certain areas, where are the boundaries, and why (or why not)? I cannot agree that this is a serious problem from a theoretical point of view. As I understand the concept of 'theory', it is no theoretical problem at all. But it is a practical problem, with serious general implications, and with ideological connotations closely bound up with the separated fields of European university studies. But if, for instance, you approach

UNIVERSITY OF WINCHESTER
LIBRARY

the study of singing activities with the background not of a folklorist but of a musicologist (as I do), you feel - since the 1970's anyway - at liberty to study what singing activities you find! The so-called problem seems closely connected with the definition of 'folklore' - and now: with the concept of 'tradition'. And I may mention that with the latest definitions of *tradition* - (Iørn Piø's and others') - this has become very broad indeed.

From a theoretical point of view, on the other hand, *any* object within musical communication *and* other cultural forms whatever they may be should be studied. What matters is how you do it.

One of the central aspects of 'tradition' is that of *time* and *continuity*. I am particularly glad that Reimund Kvideland introduced Rich. Handler's and Joc. Linnekin's article on this topic. When Handler and Linnekin maintain that "... we can no longer speak of tradition in terms of the approximate identity of some objective thing that changes while remaining the same," I quite agree. And I take their article as a good sign that this theoretical problem, which has in recent years been discussed within the humanities, is now also invading folklore. It is particularly important since in this field the concept of time, as seen in relation to the objects of research, is of a special nature.

Instead of supposing a primary identity between 'the thing then' and 'the thing now' I think it is useful to pay attention to some of the elements that denote *discontinuity*. I shall mention some quite concrete instances, well-known to many of us.

From a historical angle, for instance, we see the singing of ballads and songs carried on in new milieus, under different social and cultural circumstances, with corresponding new features in function, performance, and material. Corresponding just *how*, and reflected in *which* intricate and complex ways - well, that's our job to find out! We see, moreover, texts that are used in community-singing *'re-function'* under different social and political circumstances (Danish history is rich in such instances). And we see texts almost forgotten come to life again with new tunes - the tunes, as we know, being a most important ingredient of cultural identity from the point of view of the singers. We see that everywhere, both in oral and mixed oral-written-printed tradition, the songs take on a different quality with respect to function, *meaning* (which is important), performance, as well as the variations of texts and tunes, according to changes of generation, or even more specifically, according to the personalities of individual users.

In relation to the concept of *time*, I prefer to regard all versions of a song (recorded or not) which belong to a single individual as having their 'lives' (so to speak) within a certain *time-horizon*, which includes the situation(s) where the song was learned and which only ends with the singer herself. This set of versions, of course, may be carried on to new 'lives' under similar or different forms, and in contemporary society mass-media publications (and yet again: shifts of milieu) are very likely possibilities. Just as the singer himself very often does not realize - or does not care - what lies beyond the time-horizon of his own versions of the song, so the personal versions within a certain time-horizon may be seen as a 'thing' apart.

Tradition certainly does not grow or evolve by some inherent natural quality; but traditional elements are *used* by the members of society, individuals and groups, and thereby transformed or varied in function and material, in accordance with the changing conditions of society.

This must not be seen as if it were in conflict with the well-known observations of stability. If stability was not real, we would not be here to talk about 'tradition'.

As Danish sholars have pointed out - and possibly others - songs containing elements of *'truth'* to the singers, are preserved and carried on. I am referring especially to Thorkild Knudsen and Svend Nielsen. And this 'truth', it must be noted, does not have to be bound to the setting of the ballad, the literary meaning, or the epic core - it can be bound to a variety of elements, including the personal relationship with the person/persons in whose company the song was learned and used. The 'truth' always embodies qualities about the song that *correspond to the cultural universe and the personal world of the singer.*

Now, if we extend this concept of 'truth' to singing activities *of any kind*, communal or individual, we realize that 'truth' - or whatever we may choose to call it - is central in the process of transmission. Stable and unstable elements must be seen in relation to that. *Continuity* in tradition is as real as discontinuity, and like that, dependent on human acceptance. 'Tradition' as such, on the other hand, may be a construction, or it may be a symbolic process, as Reimund Kvideland suggests.

It will be implied, I think, in what I have said, that I do not agree with the school of 'performance' in its pure form. As far as I can see, theirs is a radically positivist line of thought, whose programme and deliberate limitations (that we cannot study what cannot be immediately observed or measured) speaks loud about the inadequacy of its views and methods. On the contrary: *how* traditional elements are accepted, refused, used, and stored, and how they carry *meaning*, also and even inside people's heads, is of the utmost importance, and we must develop our theory and methods to disclose these areas. However, it is ovbious that the *aspect of performance, among other aspects,* is a most important one, and must serve also a useful purpose of directing our attention to the present, the situations, and the activities.

Finally, I shall venture a few points on the concept of 'context'. It tends to stand as a principle or even part of a paradigm about which most scholars can agree – and at the same time, extremely vague as to contents and implications. 'Social context', in a way, is the worst. No doubt, for many scholars who are sympathetic to the 'performance' line, the only legitimate context will be the immediate social situation in a group, here and now. I am not quite certain about Reimund Kvideland's position either, when he places 'social behaviour' as *the alternative* to these 'objectivations'. He prefers the term 'singing activity' to 'performance', he says in his paper – and so do I. But then, 'performance' has special connotations, as we know, but *what* actually does 'singing activity' indicate as to theoretical views, apart from stressing the act, not the texts alone? The answers will be given, I suppose, in the near future, and I predict that there will be many kinds of answers, perhaps rather different. And the core of this has to do with how 'context' is understood.

To me 'context' implies a complex of relations, *some* of which belong to the immediate situation around the singing activities. These, however, are not only interaction and the psycho-social behaviour, but also relations that cannot be seen or measured, such as the *meaning* of texts and tunes to the singers. Reimund Kvideland states that one of our results should be to know the world view of the singers; I think that some knowledge of the singers' world view should serve also as a point of departure for the investigations: we cannot deduct world views from singing activities; but we can get to know more about both people and *singing activities as a form of ideological expression* by investigating this complex of relations.

But apart from this 'narrow' set of problems around the activity in a single group, we must consider *the conditions in the social totality*. This implies an interest, not only in the single elements of the communication chain (among which: entrepreneurs, as Reimund Kvideland writes), but in the very mechanisms of the social structure. If we do so - and try to develop our methods and concepts *in doing so* - we shall have a fair chance of approaching an understanding and explanation of 'how it all works' - in this case: the process of 'tradition'.

Discussion. Notes by *Otto Holzapfel*

Ensuing discussion focussed primarily on three aspects of Reimund Kvideland's paper: the implications of its approach for the study of early ballad traditions, the status of the 'medieval ballad', and the relevance of the term, 'singing activity'.

Kvideland agreed with Thomas Pettitt's observation that the singing activity approach, which could be seen essentially as attributing contextual factors a function in the process of artistic production, should in principle be applied to other contexts as well, such as the cultivation of 'art' songs at the courts of renaissance monarchs.

Iørn Piø remarked on the paper's somewhat belligerent stance ('you are like a warrior') and suggested that more would be convinced of the value of the 'singing activity' approach if it had more solid results to its credit; Kvideland had referred only to one book (by the Norwegian, Bjørkvold) and one Finnish article (by Pävikki Suojanen). Kvideland demurred on the belligerance, and Kirsten Sass Bak added that time was needed for such a new approach to be fully thought through and applied in substantial fashion: the results, when they appeared in due course, might well be different from those achieved so far. Svend Nielsen noted that with regard to the old ballads it would at least be a step forward to appreciate that the context was missing from the picture.

Flemming G. Andersen insisted that the concept of tradition, the passing on of material through time according to certain rules, remained central to ballad studies: discontinuity was certainly a significant phenomenon, but could be assimilated into the notion of tradition, which implied both preservation and innovation. Kirsten Sass Bak agreed: in her contribution she had emphasized discontinuity to redress the balance. Reimund Kvideland reiterated that tradition is a 'symbolic' process involving more than stability. Attention in the past had been focussed too exclusively on stability and continuity: these did not make a tradition 'genuine'.

Iørn Piø pointed out that the study of 'singing activity' in the sixteenth century was feasible only by extrapolating our knowledge of recent tradition. Svend Grundtvig himself was interested in contexts, and the insistence that a ballad is merely a text is a misunderstanding introduced by literary historians. Kvideland acknowledged that the singing activity approach, because of the lack of contextual information, could not be made to the early ballads: but the ballad is not an exclusively medieval genre: its modern traditions, including the folk-song revival, were available for study, and should be studied. To Piø's insistence that the ballad was a medieval genre Kvideland responded that he was far from decrying the kind of literary analysis which had been applied, of necessity, to the medieval texts, but that calling the ballads 'medieval' was imposing a scholarly view at odds with the realities of tradition: the bulk of the recorded texts are not medieval; ballads change over the centuries; the nineteenth century did more than just destroy the 'old ballads'; the ballads now sung in Norway have not been passed on from our great grandfathers.

Andreas Haarder saw no reason why study of singing activity in the present might not illuminate the singing activities of the past: it would at least provoke our asking new and pertinent questions of the old material. Part of the controversy may be due to the vocabulary: if 'singing activity' means more than performance, perhaps a better term could be found? Kvideland concurred in part: he had considered using the term 'social behaviour'. But it was necessary to be provocative: it was important both to ask the new questions and examine the premises of the old questions - 'tradition' was a particularly dangerous concept if not properly defined: it comprises activities, not a sequence of objectivations.

Discussion turned to the problem of using the observation of living traditions of the present to illuminate the past in the case of two specific instances, in the Faroes and Scotland. Mortan Nolsöe noted that on the Faroe Islands the old tradition of singing ballads in the ring-dance persists, but is also subject to change. Revived in dancing societies its character has changed, becoming a show for an audience: this involves departure from the older, inward-looking character of the dance, in which even physically the dancers had their backs to the audience, to a more presentational mode: there is consequently a lively debate in progress in the acceptability of these changes. With regard to Scotland, Flemming G. Andersen insisted that it was possible to identify and allow for these changes: to distinguish between the domestic performance of songs in the home and the shows put on for the folk song revival. It remains possible, and necessary, to observe the differences, and to look back from the present to the past: the retrospective value of

modern traditions should not be abandoned. Kvideland agreed that
it was possible to try, but that the process required great care:
there were many differences between modern and medieval societies, and consequently between the nature of their singing
activities, so we should be careful not to mix them together.

Sven-Bertil Jansson found this too sceptical: the ballad has a
history, and Swedish editorial practice places the ballad in a
medieval context. It is an unavoidable consequence that we have
little information about the singing activity aspect, and that with
so few medieval texts available we have to print what is available.
For Reimund Kvideland this was an inappropriate perspective: it
led to the exclusion of material not deemed 'medieval', applied
undocumented notions on the nature of tradition, assigned an
arbitrary value to age, and focussed on objectivations rather than
activities.

Viggo Hjørnager Pedersen wondered why 'objectivation' should
be used in such a pejorative fashion: there was an object in the
activity after all: there would be little 'singing activity' without
the songs; activity and objectivation are simply two aspects of the
same phenomenon. Kvideland remarked that he was using 'objectivation' in the sense applied by Karl Popper. The problem was
scholarship had hitherto concentrated exclusively on the objectivations: description of the processes involved were merely added as
a decoration. Iørn Piø noted that in essence Kvideland was recom-
mending a folkloristic approach to the ballads (as opposed to a
literary one). Andreas Haarder reiterated that activity implied
being active with something: both aspects merited attention in
research.

Thomas Pettitt wondered why there was so much scepticism
about studying the old texts in relation to the singing activities of
their own times: were there no contextual sources for the late-
medieval and early-modern periods in Scandinavia? Iørn Piø remarked that there were plenty of contexts, but no texts. Svend
Nielsen noted there was a little information, and that more might
be uncovered. Tore Nyberg insisted that the information was there
if the effort were made to discover it: references to singing
activities occur in regulations and homiletic material as in local
and ecclesiastical sources. Vésteinn Ólason was less encouraging
with regard to early contextual material in Iceland: some descrip-
tions of dancing for example, but that was not sufficient.

Session 2

Traditional Patterns and the Religious Ballads

Written paper
BY DAVID BUCHAN

The variety of the human mind and the individuality of ballad scholars have ensured that more than one concept of ballad tradition has existed. Nevertheless, certain tendencies have pervaded scholarship and a major one has been the tendency to conceive of tradition as largely a matter of ballad tradition. This is unfortunate since balladry, for a rounded understanding, needs to be seen as one genre within the entire folk tradition, and since ballad scholars will benefit greatly from the approaches and discoveries of research in folkloristics at large. The contextualist approach has much to offer, as has modern performance and communication theory, as Reimund Kvideland has recently demonstrated.1) Many of the modern approaches, however, operate best in synchronic application, and adjustments have to be made for balladry with its pronouncedly diachronic range; the texts of ballad tradition, for example, can not be discarded as major evidence since for the diachronic perspective they constitute our basic data. But modern scholarship in the contiguous genres of tradition may provide new analytic means for the better understanding of these texts.

The texts of ballad tradition exhibit many patterns, and these supply insight into the relationship of text to traditional processes. The many structural and verbal patternings, for instance, demonstrate the methods of composition and transmission. But patternings reveal not just how the ballad is told but *what* essentially is

1. "Folk Ballad and Song", Trends in Nordic Tradition Research, eds. Lauri Honko and Pekka Laaksonen, Studia Fennica 27 (Helsinki: Suomalaisen Kirjallisuuden Seura, 1983), pp.177-183.

told. Some narrative patterns are cross-generic, like the Return of Hero after Long Absence pattern which exemplifies the Tension of Essences concept 2) and which appears in "Hind Horn" (17), "Young Beichan" (53), and "The Kitchie-Boy" (252). Other patterns of actors and action permeate, and may indeed define, the subgenres that make up the genre of balladry. Is there, then, a methodological approach from modern folkloristic scholarship with which to explore the patternings of subgenres so as to illuminate both the processes of tradition and the meanings of the textual material? The answer to such a rhetorical question has to be "yes"; the method is that of talerole analysis. From now on, the paper utilises the method of talerole analysis developed by Vladimir Propp, in his research into Russian wonder tales, for an investigation of the patternings in the subgenre of Religious ballads.3)

Propp's concept is simplicity itself. He suggests that one employ a bilevel analytic perspective and consider not only the character on the concrete level but also, on the abstract level, the talerole whose function the character fulfils. The Russian wonder tale, he discovered, has seven taleroles for the entire genre. Anglophone scholarship in general has been slow to take up Propp's percept because the translation into English of Propp's Russian confused his statements on the subject. In an earlier attempt to remedy the deficiency by applying talerole analysis to balladry I found that the norm for most of the ballad subgenres is a three-talerole pattern.4)

The Religious ballads were chosen to exemplify the method for a cluster of reasons: as with most minor subgenres not a great deal has been written on them; a small group, they are reasonably compassable for present purposes; half of them have Nordic

2. Albert B. Lord, The Singer of Tales (Cambridge, Mass: Harvard U.P., 1960), pp. 97-98, 120-123.
3. Vladimir Propp, Morphology of the Folktale, 2nd rev. ed., trans. L. Scott and rev. L.A. Wagner (Austin: University of Texas Press, 1968), pp. 79-83; Heda Jason and Dimitri Segal, "The Problem of 'Tale Role' and 'Character' in Propp's Work", Patterns in Oral Literature, eds. Jason and Segal (The Hague: Mouton, 1977), pp. 313-320.
4. "Propp's Tale Role and a Ballad Repertoire", Journal of American Folklore, 95 (1982), 159-172.

analogues;5) and they are an area of interest of Mr. Pettitt, who has written on "St. Stephen and Herod" in *The Ballad as Narrative*.6) The subgenre comprises eight types. In "The Maid and the Palmer" (21), Mary Magdalen (actually a composite figure involving also the Woman of Samaria) is confronted with her unchastity and the murders of her children by an "old palmer" who, as Jesus, then assigns her penances after which, it is clear in Scandinavian tradition, she will ascend to heaven.7) Brown Robyn (in 57) impedes the progress of his ship because, he confesses when confronted by his men, he has committed incest; they throw him overboard and the Blessed Virgin takes him up to heaven. In "Dives and Lazarus" (56), Dives treats the poor beggar Lazarus with cruel callousness, but is transported to the pains of hell while Lazarus has "a place prepared in heaven,/To sit on an angel's knee". "The Bitter Withy" ironically has Jesus commit the sin, that of drowning through misuse of his miraculous powers three lords' sons who scorn his lowliness, and then be subjected to earthly justice.8) In "St. Stephen and Herod" (22) Herod declares that Stephen's words on the birth of Christ have as much likelihood as a cooked capon

5.	CH21: <u>TSB</u> B16; CH22: <u>TSB</u> B8; CH55: <u>TSB</u> B3; CH57: <u>TSB</u> D360, 361. (TSB = <u>The Types of the Scandinavian Medieval Ballad</u>, eds. Bengt R. Jonsson, Svale Solheim and Eva Danielson (Stockholm and Oslo, 1978).)

6.	"'St. Stephen and Herod' and the Songs of the Sloane Manuscript", <u>The Ballad as Narrative</u>, eds. Flemming G. Andersen, Otto Holzapfel, and Thomas Pettitt (Odense: Odense University Press, 1982), pp. 19-38.

7.	See in addition to the version and fragment in Child: David Buchan, "The Maid, the Palmer, and the Cruel Mother", <u>The Malahat Review</u>, 3 (1967), 98-107; Sean Corcoran, "Two Songs", <u>Ceol</u>, 3 (1969), 66-70; Tom Munnelly, "The Man and his Music ... John Reilly", <u>Ceol</u>, 4 (1972), 2-8; Bertrand Bronson, <u>The Traditional Tunes of the Child Ballads</u>, IV (Princeton: Princeton University Press, 1972), 457-459.

8.	Frank Sidgwick, "The Bitter Withy", <u>Notes and Queries</u>, ser. 10, vol. IV (1905), 84-85; Gordon Hall Gerould, "The Ballad of the Bitter Withy", <u>PMLA</u>, 23 (1908), 141-167; Ella M. Leather et al., "Carols from Herefordshire", <u>Journal of the Folk-Song Society</u>, 4 (1910-1913), 29-47.

has of crowing, and is confounded by the miraculous crowing, but has Stephen stoned to death. In "The Cherry-Tree Carol" (54) when Mary says she is pregnant and asks for a cherry, Joseph responds that whoever made her pregnant can perform that service, and then Jesus has the cherry-tree miraculously bow down, before prophesying his own death. Within the framework of a dialogue between two birds "The Carnal and the Crane" (55) has Herod persecute the Holy Family until eventually foiled by the miracle of the instantaneous harvest; the Slaughter of the Innocents, however, has taken place. Judas (in 23) sells Jesus to Pilate for thirty pieces of silver and is confounded by Jesus' miraculous knowledge of the betrayal, which is followed by a prophecy of another betrayal, that of Peter.9)

The Religious ballads contain a relationship involving one or more biblical or morally didactic figures in an adversarial tension which leads to divine or miraculous intercession. The stories deal with the commission, or revelation, of a sin and the subsequent divine reaction. The three taleroles are: Sinner, Adversary, Interceder; the Sinner is, naturally, the person who commits or has committed a sin; the Adversary is the other person, or persons, appositional in the relationship to the Sinner; and the Interceder provides the divine reaction to the commission of the sin. Schematically depicted, the taleroles and characters stand as follows:

9.   Some essays on the types of the subgenre are: Edith Batho, "The Life of Christ in the Ballads", Essays and Studies. . . of the English Association, 9 (1924), 70-97; Paul Franklin Baum, "The English Ballad of Judas Iscariot", PMLA, 31 (1916), 181-189; Mollie McCabe, "A Rewritten Version of 'The Carnal and the Crane' (Child 55)", Folk Music Journal, 4:5 (1984), 528-538; Pamela L. Royston, "'The Cherry-Tree Carol': Its Sources and Analogues", Folklore Forum, 15 (1982), 1-16.

TYPE

TALEROLE		SINNER	ADVERSARY	INTERCEDER
CHARACTER:	21	Mary Magdalen	"palmer"	Jesus
	57	H	H men	BVM
	56	Dives	Lazarus	Holy Ghost
	TBW	Jesus	3H	Mary
	22	Herod	St. Stephen	Holy Ghost
	54	Joseph	Mary	Jesus
	55	Herod	Holy Family	Holy Ghost
			Wise Men	Jesus
			husbandman	
	23	Judas	Pilate	Jesus
		Judas Sr.	Judas	

Abbreviations:	H	:	he, male character
	H men	:	H's men
	Sr	:	sister
	BVM	:	Blessed Virgin Mary
	TBW	:	"The Bitter Withy"

The characters occupying the taleroles include two members of the Trinity, Jesus and the Holy Ghost, and the Blessed Virgin Mary, who also appears with Joseph and the young Jesus as a member of the Holy Family; people from Jesus' life story, Herod, the Wise Men, Mary Magdalen (cum-Woman of Samaria), Pilate, and Judas (together with a sister); a saint from a Nativity legend, two men from a parable in Luke,10) and in one ballad (57) a ship's captain and his crew.

As Propp found in the wonder tale, there is not always a straight one-on-one relationship for character and talerole. Sometimes one character can occupy more than one talerole, as in 21, where Jesus as the "old palmer" fills the Adversary role before assuming that of the Interceder. Conversely, one talerole may be occupied by more than one character, as in 55, where Herod's hostility to the Holy Family expresses itself in scenes with the Wise Men and the husbandman. This example may serve to illustrate how the talerole method of structuralist analysis has a

10. Luke 16:19-31.

paradigmatic component. The same character may fill different roles in different stories, when, for example, Mary appears as both Adversary and Interceder, or Jesus appears as all three. The schema for this subgenre differs from that for most, since, while in other subgenres the schemas have a preponderance of characters labelled H, S, HM, SF, V, etc. (leading male character, leading female character, H's mother, S's father, villain) where the names are of little significance, here the subgenre is populated largely by the very specific characters of Christian mythology whose names are of considerable significance. Only "Brown Robyn's Confession" (57) contains for two of the three taleroles characters without mythological import. This subgenre has one other distinguishing feature. In three of the stories the function of the Interceder talerole is not fulfilled by a named character but is nevertheless accomplished by divine agency: in "St. Stephen and Herod" (22) and "The Carnal and the Crane" (55) the roasted cock or capon crows "By the work of God's own hand" (55:11.2); and in "Dives and Lazarus" (56) the serpents and angels that escort the one to hell and the other to heaven do so at divine instigation. In these three types where the function of the talerole is fulfilled by divine agency the Holy Ghost has been designated the Interceder.

When the taleroles are described more particularly, in terms of the specific types, they indicate the various manifestations of the general pattern in the individual stories:

Talerole 1

Sinner 21	: Mary Magdalen	: fornicator, murderer
Sinner 57	: H	: committer of incest
Sinner 56	: Dives	: cruelly selfish man
Sinner TBW	: Jesus	: murderer
Sinner 22	: Herod	: unbeliever, murderer
Sinner 54	: Joseph	: unbeliever, accuser
Sinner 55	: Herod	: persecutor, murderer
Sinner 23	: Judas	: betrayer

Talerole 2

| Adversary 21 | : "palmer" | : confronter with sin |
| Adversary 57 | : H men | : confronters with the fact of having sinned |

Adversary 56	:	Lazarus	:	victim, of cruel treatment
Adversary TBW	:	3 H	:	victims, of murder
Adversary 22	:	St. Stephen	:	victim, of murder; martyr
Adversary 54	:	Mary	:	innocent accused
Adversary 55	:	Holy Family	:	intended victims, persecuted
Adversary 23	:	Pilate	:	tempter

Talerole 3

Interceder 21	:	Jesus	:	dispenser of divine justice
Interceder 57	:	BVM	:	dispenser of divine justice
Interceder 56	:	Holy Ghost	:	dispenser of divine justice
Interceder TBW	:	Mary	:	dispenser of human justice
Interceder 22	:	Holy Ghost	:	justifier of belief through a miracle
Interceder 54	:	Jesus	:	justifier of belief through a miracle
Interceder 55	:	Holy Ghost	:	justifier of belief and protector of the Holy Family through miracles
Interceder 23	:	Jesus	:	justifier of belief in His divinity through miraculous knowledge

From the delineation of the actors in the stories one can proceed to lay out the pattern of action and divine reaction that animates the subgenre. Schematically depicted, the basic patterns of the eight types stand thus:

21	Confrontation with past sin leads to divine justice: penance and redemption
57	Confrontation with, and confession of, past sin lead to earthly justice and then divine justice: redemption
56	Sin of cruel selfishness leads to divine justice: damnation (and salvation for the victim)
TBW	Sin of murder (a misuse of miraculous powers) leads to earthly justice
22	Sin of unbelief is confounded by a miracle; a martyrdom follows

54	Sin of unbelief is confounded by a miracle; a prophecy of death and resurrection follows
55	Sin of unbelief and attempted persecution are confounded by miracles; murders follow
23	Sin of betrayal is revealed by miraculous knowledge; a prophecy of another betrayal (and, by implication, death) follows

There emerges from this schema a picture of two groupings, with each group governed by the basic pattern whereby the commission or revelation of a sin generates a divine reaction. Where the sins of the first group, however, are those of fornication, incest, murder, and selfishness, those of the second group are unbelief and betrayal (which could possibly be construed as a form of unbelief). The first group is concerned centrally with sin and divine justice. In each of types 21, 57, and 56 an individual - two sinners and a blameless man - achieves salvation, while in 56 the sinner antithetical to the blameless man is consigned to damnation. In "The Maid and the Palmer" the sinner attains redemption through penance; in "Brown Robyn's Confession" the sinner attains redemption through "fair confession"; and in "Dives and Lazarus" Lazarus ascends to heaven after a life of blameless suffering whereas the incorrigible sinner Dives descends to Hell there to perceive, too late, the error of his ways. Divine justice, then, shows as God's mercy for sinners who confess or repent and for those who, though despised and rejected, lead unblemished lives, and, on the other hand, as God's judgment on the sinner who remains obdurate. "The Bitter Withy" has an ironic inversion of the pattern in that Jesus is the sinner and exercises divine power during the commission of the sin, to receive as his desert earthly justice; instead of human action followed by divine reaction, there is divine action followed by human reaction.

The second group is concerned centrally with the sin of unbelief and the countering expression of divine power in miracles, all juxtaposed with accounts of the killing of the innocent (a saint-martyr, Jesus, the Innocents). The juxtaposition provides a notable element in the patterning for it balances in cautionary fashion the assertion of God's omnipotence with the reminder that in this world the innocent do get killed; an awkward theological point is rendered in comprehensible narrative terms. The sin of unbelief which Herod commits in 22 and 55 is compounded in the latter by his persecution of the Holy Family, and the miracles in these types are balanced by the martyrdom of St. Stephen and the Massacre of the Innocents. Type 54 portrays the mildest of the sins in a gentle variation of the theme for here the sin of unbelief takes the form of Joseph's inability to accept the Immaculate Conception; the miracle is followed by an angel's prophecy of Christ's birth in a number of versions, before Jesus Himself prophesies His death and, yet another balancing element, His resurrection. In "Judas" (23) can be discerned the essential line of the pattern, in that his sin of betrayal is revealed and confounded by miraculous knowledge, and followed by the prophecy of another betrayal (Peter's) and, through implication, the death of Christ; but the pattern here is not as fully realised as in the other types. The miraculous element is not confined to the second grouping: it appears also, ironically deployed, in "The Bitter Withy", while in "Dives and Lazarus" at the standard point in the action - at the end of the interaction of Sinner and Adversary - occurs the episode where the men and the dogs sent to harass Lazarus have no power to whip or to bite, which could be interpreted as a miraculous intervention. In the second grouping, then, unbelief is countered by a miracle which is in turn balanced by guiltless death. The underlying concern is with the necessity of faith, which is the converse of unbelief and which demands the acceptance of both miracles and the death of the innocent. The two groupings deal with human sin and divine mercy, mortal peccancy and God's power, the possibility that the guilty may achieve salvation in the next life and the possibility that the innocent may perish in this life, but the emphasis in one is on divine justice and in the other on faith.

Certain thematic devices help to convey these weighty concerns in a lively and acceptable narrative form for a popular audience. The members of the Holy Family are portrayed in very human fashion: in "The Bitter Withy" Jesus appears as a mischievous boy and Mary as a chastising mother; in "The Cherry-Tree Carol" Joseph appears as an old man doubting the fidelity of his young wife and Mary appears as a pregnant woman with the stereotypical craving for a particular taste. Even Judas is presented in a humanly sympathetic light as someone first sinned against before sinning. Again, in many of the ballads there exists a contrast between wealth and poverty, rank and lowliness, where sympathies obviously reside with the less fortunate. This shows most obviously in the ballad about the poor man welcomed into heaven and the rich man denied access, but occurs also in the stress on Jesus' lowliness in 54B, C, D, 55, and "The Bitter Withy." Another thematic device which brings the stories closely home is the presentation in 22 and 23 of relationships in lord-and-servant terms. These thematic devices not only render the stories more accessible but also highlight Christ's duality, for He appears as both Our Lord and the Suffering Servant.

Elucidation of the talerole patterns and the thematic patterns establishes certain constants in the subgenre, which provides a perspective from which to review the subgeneric status of certain pieces with claims to inclusion. "The Bitter Withy", with the three taleroles and the straightforward inversion of the main pattern of action, merits inclusion. The "Corpus Christi" carol, on the other hand, possesses none of the features of the subgenre.11) "The Holy Well" I have not included because it seems a sentimental variation on the theme of "The Bitter Withy" which is itself a variation on the main pattern: all of which takes one rather far from the centre; but certainly a case for its inclusion could be made out.12) And how do the subgeneric features bear on the vexed question of Type 23's status? "Judas", as we have seen, contains the central taleroles and the central pattern in a strongly latent rather than fully realised fashion. On balance this evidence would tend to confirm rather than deny its traditionality, but, most of all, it would support the view that "Judas" is a proto-ballad, that is, it is a story being told in a balladic mode which is just evolving into maturity.

The talerole patterns also enable one to perceive the hybrids, the types or versions which have elements of more than one genre. "Bonnie Annie" (24), for example, has the Sinner and Adversary taleroles but lacks the Interceder. The C text of "The Wife of Usher's Well" (79) and the A text of "Leesome Brand" (15) conversely lack the Sinner and Adversary taleroles but have the Interceder. Once the relationship is established, then other linkings

11. M.J.C. Hodgart, The Ballads, 2nd ed. (London: Hutchinson, 1962), pp. 38-41; Richard L. Greene, The Early English Carols, 2nd rev. ed. (Oxford: Oxford U.P., 1977), pp. 195- 197.
12. Leather et al., 26-28; Cecil Sharp, "Carols. 1 -- 'The Holy Well'", Journal of the Folk-Song Society, V (1914-1917), 1-6.

become clear; 15A, 24, and 57, for example, share a quite noteworthy batch of motifs.

Consideration of the patterns indicates the major functions of the subgenre. In places the subgenre is overtly or implicitly homiletic. Where in "The Maid and the Palmer" the value of penance is stressed, in "Brown Robyn's Confession" it is the value of confession:

> 'It's for nae honour ye did to me, Brown Robyn,
>   It's for nae guid ye did to mee;
> But a' is for your fair confession
>   You've made upon the sea.'   (57: 9)

Where "Dives and Lazarus" exemplifies forcefully the injunction to love thy neighbour, "The Carnal and the Crane" proffers a direct moral:

> There's thousands of children young
>   Which for his sake did die;
> Do not forbid those little ones,
>   And do not them deny.   (55: 29)

The subgenre presents the life of Jesus to a popular audience in a narratively entertaining manner; in doing so it depicts Jesus both as God, as merciful Redeemer, and as man, whether as Suffering Servant or as mischievous boy. The subgenre also portrays and celebrates the operation of the divine force in the universe, while dealing in accessible narrative terms with such theological concepts as justice and faith. All in all, the subgenre functions to reinforce and validate belief: belief in God and His powers, in Jesus His son, and in the mythic significance of the Holy Family and the figures in their story. What analysis reveals, then, are not just abstract "literary" patterns but actual cultural concerns of the participants in the ballad tradition.

The ballad genre, I have suggested elsewhere, concerns itself essentially with relationships. What kind of relationship lies at the heart of this subgenre with its taleroles of Sinner, Adversary, and Interceder? When one articulates the relations of the taleroles a basic pattern emerges: a sin of the Sinner is committed upon or revealed by the Adversary and given eschatological significance by the reaction of the Interceder. The situation here is rather more complex than in most subgenres: here the relationship between Sinner and Adversary is succeeded by the relationship of the Interceder to either or both of that pair; the human behaviour affecting the initial relationship is put into eschatological perspective by the divine representative in the second relationship. If, then, the concern is with human behaviour and divine reactions to it, the subgenre deals centrally with the relationship of mortals to God.

The method of talerole analysis can delineate the distinguishing features of a subgenre - its actors, its action, and their significance. By determining, like all useful structuralist methods, the constants and the variables, it can show with some precision the relationship of the types within a subgenre and at the same time the individuality of the different types. It can be used to assess types of dubious generic status and to uncover the links between one subgenre and another through the types with talerole hybrids. And it can reveal the cultural concerns fundamental to the subgenre. This is not to claim that standard analysis could not also achieve some of the same ends, simply that talerole analysis does bring into focus certain essential matters, and thereby facilitates the understanding of others. Folkloristic scholarship in general, not ballad scholarship, has furnished this useful methodological tool. Developed for one genre but applicable to other folklore genres, talerole analysis illuminates the narrative and thematic patterns intrinsic to balladry that parallel the structural and verbal patterns, and in consequence sheds some interesting light on the interrelationships of texts, patterns, and tradition.

Memorial University of Newfoundland.

Oral presentation by *David Buchan*

My printed paper takes an empirical approach to our topic, in order to provide a concrete basis for discussion. It is intended, first, to demonstrate the existence of certain patterns in balladry; second, and complementarily, to show the availability of a methodological tool for the analysis of such patterns; and, third, to raise issues of significance deriving from these patterns for the debate on the concept of tradition.

The methodological perspective is supplied by Propp's concept of the talerole, explained on p. 28 in this fashion: "He suggests that one employ a bilevel analytic perspective and consider not only the character on the concrete level but also, on the abstract level, the talerole whose function the character fulfils." This perspective enables one to distinguish in the subgenre under discussion the three taleroles of Sinner, Adversary, and Interceder, which in turn lead to the perceiving of a basic pattern ("whereby the commission or revelation of a sin generates a divine reaction") and certain constants in the themes. These thematic constants indicate the cultural concerns and indeed the cultural functioning of this ballad subgenre.

Now, the debate. In the past, tradition tended to be seen in terms of its actual productions. In the more recent past has emerged an understanding of the need for tradition to be seen in terms of people, and the processes that link people and their productions. The study of tradition would become a dehumanised affair if we were to neglect the individual, the group, and their relations to their culture and their society. The individual, as creator and performer, and the group, as audience, comprise the participants in the performance context (or "situational context" in Bausinger's phrase), a context which in turn has to be seen in terms of the wider socio-cultural contexts.

The debate has been given a very precise focus for the Symposium by the title of Reimund Kvideland's paper: "Tradition: Objectivations or Social Behaviour?" The one term there indicates that folkloristics has for one parent literary study, and the other that folkloristics has for the other parent anthropology. But folkloristics, I would suggest, is neither literary study nor anthropology but an adult discipline in its own right, which amalgamates

genes from both parents. Tradition, then, is neither "objectivations" nor "social behaviour" alone; it comprehends both. Folkloristics differentiates itself from both its parents by not concerning
itself primarily or exclusively with, on the one hand, texts, and on
the other, culture; it deals distinctively with the artefact in
culture (and the sociofact, and the mentifact, and many other
facts).

If, however, folkloristics is regarded as a funny kind of literary
study and ballads looked on as wilfully perverse poems which do not
adhere to standard critical rules, then studies of individual texts
will produce only limited gains, with much speculation, and aesthetic discussion of doubtful value. If folkloristics is regarded as a
funny kind of anthropology and ballads looked on only as things
which happen during a set of human interactions that constitute
the really important data for understanding of social groups, then
again the studies will be of limited usefulness. If, however,
folkloristics is regarded as an autonomous discipline, whose primary concern is not the artefact alone, or the socio-cultural
ambience alone, but the interrelationship of the artefact and
culture, then ballad studies concerned with the interrelationship of
texts and contexts will tend rather to produce results of a
fruitfully holistic nature which, incidentally, should be of both
material and methodological use for literary scholars and anthro-
pologists. It is necessary, then, to study the socio-cultural and
performance contexts, particularly for the illumination they cast
on the artefacts; and conversely to study the artefacts as expressive forms, particularly for the illumination they cast on their
socio-cultural matrix. Clearly the researcher can start from either
direction, depending on the evidential material available.

The performance event or the "singing activity" requires our
attention, but I would suggest that the central feature of the event
is the communicative activity which goes on. The communicative
activity engenders our interest both because of the creativity of
the performing individual and because of its cultural meanings for
the group. For both topics, one can learn from the texts that are
the major means of communication, since the texts are full of
patterns (indicative of the "systems and codes" referred to by
Vésteinn Ólason); some of these patterns illuminate the creativity
of the composition, others illuminate actual cultural concerns and
meanings. At the heart of the performance event, then, are the

texts which, when analysed folkloristically, reveal the communicative processes involving the event's participants and their socio-cultural matrix.

The printed paper is an attempt to show, from a subgenre of ballads largely without information about performance contexts, how the patterns that permeate tradition may, with a useful folkloristic method, disclose how the expressive forms of traditional culture functioned within traditional culture. The concern lies not with the artefact *qua* artefact, but with the artefact in culture.

Opposition by *Thomas Pettitt*

Discussion of the theoretical basis of tale-role analysis may be
avoided, since Professor Buchan has already demonstrated what is
more important, its practical feasibility, in an earlier study of
'Propp's Tale Role and a Ballad Repertoire', published in the
Journal of American Folklore in 1982. The repertoire concerned
was that of the celebrated 18th century Scottish singer, Mrs.
Brown of Falkland, and analysis revealed the suitability of talerole configurations as a means of defining and characterizing the
subgenres of balladry. Response to the present paper can therefore
be more specific and more concrete, and focus on, firstly, the
specific problems of applying tale-role analysis to a single subgenre, and specifically the religious ballads; secondly, in view of
the general theme of the conference, perspectives in relation to
ballad tradition: the implications of Professor Buchan's insights for
an understanding of ballad tradition, and conversely the significance of ballad tradition for our assessment of Professor Buchan's
insights.
      (The following comments were illustrated by reference to a
handout providing a number of ballads and related texts.)

1. Tale-Role Analysis and the Religious Ballads

The religious ballads are a significant but much neglected subgenre, which probably loomed larger in early tradition than the few
surviving texts do in the standard collections. It is therefore
appropriate that any technique of analysis should sooner or later be
tried on them, and in this instance it is intriguing that when Bruce
A. Beattie attempted to analyse a group of Child ballads according
to Propp's narrative functions, it was precisely and exclusively the
religious ballads which failed to respond to the treatment. ("Traditional Structures and the Structure of Tradition: A Functional
System of Ballad Classification", in *Ballads and Ballad Research*,
ed. Patricia Conroy, Seattle, 1978).
      Professor Buchan does not make explicit his criteria for the
initial selection of the material to be subjected for analysis. The
ballads derive from manuscripts, broadsides, songbooks and oral

tradition, and are not restricted to the Child canon: the initial selection includes "The Bitter Withy" (but not other non-Child ballads such as "The Holy Well" and "The Seven Virgins"). Conversely the selection excludes Child 155, "Sir Hugh, or the Jews Daughter" which has a strong claim to be included among the religious ballads. And the ballad status of two of the selections, furthermore, "Judas" and "The Carnal and the Crane", is doubtful. Given the limited corpus of eight songs chosen for study, the exclusion of a couple of them, or the inclusion of three or four others, might have had a significant influence on the results. Indeed the impact of the study could have been greatly enhanced by selection of a miscellany of more or less religious narrative songs, both ballads and non-ballads (e.g. carols), and seeing if tale-role analysis could effectively sort them out.

Of the songs excluded here, Professor Buchan has in fact already examined "Sir Hugh", as it occurs in Mrs. Brown's repertoire. In his earlier study he observes that it does not fit completely into any of the other sub-genres, and remarks, significantly, that this "may exemplify how a story of non-traditional provenance is adapted to a traditional genre" (*JAF*, 95 (1982), p. 167). Indeed one of the peculiar problems and one of the unique opportunities in dealing with the religious ballads is that the holy legends they tell exist independently, and in most cases originate, in other non-balladic, narrative forms, providing the chance of observing how the ballad's way of telling a story differs from the telling of the same story in other genres, and of testing whether tale-role analysis can detect these generic differences. Take for instance the story of Dives and Lazarus, as told in the ballad of that title (Child 56), in the traditional non-ballad song "Lazarus" (e.g. Bronson, *The Traditional Tunes of the Child Ballads*, No. 56.10), and in *St Luke's Gospel* ch. XVI. Of these three renditions of the story, only "Dives and Lazarus" is a ballad: but it is so distinguished not because of the tale-roles, which are identical in all three forms, but because of its verbal handling of the story, for example using a complex pattern of repetitions. Tale-role analysis may distinguish between ballad sub-genres; it apparently cannot distinguish between ballads and other narrative forms.

2. Tale-Role Analysis and Ballad Tradition

Professor Buchan's paper discusses ballads rather than specific ballad-texts, and therefore does not allow sufficiently for the textual changes ballads undergo in the course of tradition. Even limited and simple textual additions, subtractions and substitutions can have significant impact on the tales and the tale-roles. Such changes are capable of transferring a ballad from one sub-genre to another. "The Wife of Usher's Well" for instance (Child 79), tells the story of a mother whose three sons die away from home. In some renditions (e.g. Bronson 79.3) the mother threatens God that she will abjure her faith if her sons do not return; God complies, but their brief visit must be construed as a punishment for her temerity: this is a religious ballad by Professor Buchan's definition. In other versions (e.g. Bronson 79.25) the mother earnestly and sincerely prays to God, and their return, though brief, is a reward for her faith: this is a religious ballad by any definition other than Professor Buchan's. In a third rendition (e.g. Bronson 79.10), thanks largely to the omission of a couple of stanzas, the mother does not know they are dead; only when they return (apparently for the Christmas holidays) does their odd speech and behaviour reveal the awful truth: this is not a religious ballad by any definition.

A central problem in dealing with multi-textual genres like the traditional ballad is deciding if analysis is applied to, and valid for, a particular version of the ballad concerned, all the available versions, or some conglomerate of conveniently selected bits and pieces. Professor Buchan comes perilously close to the last procedure in discussing Child 21, "The Maid and the Palmer", offering the following thematic summary: "Confrontation with past sin leads to divine justice: penance and redemption" (p. 33). The redemption of the Maiden is less than certain in the only complete version of this ballad (Child 21A) and clearly ruled out in the fragmentary B-text in Child. It is revealed in his narrative summary (p. 29) that Professor Buchan has in fact supplied the happy ending from "Scandinavian tradition": a potentially hazardous procedure. Tale-role analysis, any kind of analysis, should be based on a single, specified text of a ballad, and, until the other versions are examined the results should be taken as valid for that text alone: this is the only safe way to approach a tradition in which the texts won't stand still. That the approach may have significant implications for the kind of analysis undertaken by Professor Buchan may be finally illustrated by a glance at "The Cherry Tree Carol" (Child 54). Professor Buchan's summary and analysis of this ballad fit four of the texts provided by Child and Bronson, which have Mary's request for cherries, Joseph's surly response, and the intervention of Jesus from the womb, who orders the tree to bow down, before prophesying his death and resurrection. But the remaining 15 texts all vary in one or more significant ways from this rendition of the story. In eight texts there is no concluding prophecy; in seven Jesus prophesies his birth, not his death. In one version, Mary is not pregnant, so Joseph has nothing to say about it, and when Jesus intervenes it is as a Child, not a miraculously loquacious foetus, and in a domestic quarrel rather than a theological controversy. In one version it is God who intervenes to make the tree bow down, in another Mary does so, and in a third (perhaps it had to be a Canadian version) the tree decides to do so of its own volition. And these are not, generally speaking, garblings of the legend: each telling is coherent in its own way; tradition has changed the story, not sung it to pieces, but in the process has played havoc with the tale-roles.

Discussion. Notes by *Flemming G. Andersen*

In response to Thomas Pettitt's point of criticism that he used conglomerates of texts for his talerole analysis where really we should analyse *versions* of texts David Buchan observed that this was quite deliberate. Not even with "The Maid and the Palmer" where Thomas Pettitt had referred to the only version known to him, did he confine his analysis to a single text. Apart from the nineteenth century Scottish version there are some Irish versions, recorded within the last fifteen years, and all these versions should be taken into account. Buchan noted that the versions of "The Wife of Usher's Well", on the other hand, showed the unhappiness with the folkloristic concept of 'type'. A type of any given story has to be seen in its verbal form (cf. Aarne-Thompson), but is also an intellectual abstraction of the body of versions. And we cannot look at this intellectual abstract in verbal form. Individual judgements can be faulty, but the concept is a basic one in folkloristics. As concerns "Dives and Lazarus" David Buchan pointed out that the genre takes in certain stories because they are conformable to the ballad form.

Michel Olsen intervened to note that according to Propp folk tales can be subdivided into many categories, and that Propp himself discarded what was not 'Zauber Märchen'. He claimed that not all religious ballads should be analysed in the manner presented, while Buchan argued that there are no other religious songs to be studied than the ones referred to. There may be some individual songs, Middle English carols, etc., but having spot-checked the area he was very doubtful that they would exhibit the same talerole patterns that we find in the classical ballads.

Thomas Pettitt agreed that relevant material is sparse in the carols and legends, but restated his misgivings about the talerole analysis - "Dives and Lazarus" has the same talerole pattern that we find in the gospel according to St. Luke, while "The Cherry Tree Carol" tells its story differently from the prose legend. The analysis should take this into account.

Asked by Marianne Børch why he did not include "Sir Hugh" in his analysis Buchan replied that he had already written about "Sir Hugh" in a previous study ["Propp's Tale Role and a Ballad Repertoire"], and there it had showed that this ballad is a hybrid. "Sir

Hugh" is responsive to any secondary subgeneric pattern; it is totally on its own.

Returning to the question of 'type' Thomas Pettitt argued that if our analysis concerns only intellectual abstractions we can establish no 'real' contexts, and consequently there will be a contradiction between approach and matter in folklore studies. Prompted by this statement Vésteinn Ólason maintained that we must make abstractions in order to be able to make generalizations, but granted that this is somewhat unsatisfactory since we are then creating the object we are dealing with.

Viggo Hjørnager Pedersen questioned the appropriateness of giving up the notion of version and asked how we can then determine that we are dealing with the same ballad, as for instance in the case of the "Dives and Lazarus"-texts. Referring to Ólason's observations Buchan replied that we need generalizations. With the concept of type we construct a generalization of the story, and hereby we are able to see the minor variations. He did not think that it would disturb the integrity of the generalization that we knew it had been constructed, but pointed out that absolutism is dangerous.

Observing that a number of generalizations can be made on any material Viggo Hjørnager Pedersen wanted to know which of these would be the more correct, and Buchan observed that folk narratives are easier to deal with than ballads because we there have the Aarne-Thompson index, on which everybody agrees.

Andreas Haarder intervened to state that we have to generalize, and that this was all right as long as we knew the shortcomings of it. He went on to inquire about the delimitation of 'themes' and questioned the notion of 'religious ballads' - in "The Wife of Usher's Well" one version contains a curse, another a prayer; would this make one secular, and the other religious?

David Buchan took the point, and agreed that he must elaborate on his method of analysis. There are different settings, and different elements are being stressed in particular circumstances. "The Wife of Usher's Well" seems to belong to the subgeneric group of 'revenant ballads'. He suggested that the final result of the method may be the classification of ballads.

Advocating a different approach Thomas Pettitt suggested that we might take a rag-bag of material and then see what was essential to it. Buchan found this approach valid, and noted that ballads as religious stories also belong to the religious material; which means that their features may belong to various subgroups. He stated that the area of legend has tremendously interesting patterns - shipwreck legends turn up surprisingly repetitive patterns which can be analysed in Proppian terms. Pettitt observed that we find medieval legends with the same talerole configurations as had been established for the religious ballads.

Marianne Børch returned to Buchan's introductory remarks concerning the inappropriateness of applying literary methods to the field of traditional balladry, and asked whether ballads *are* bad literature. In response Buchan observed that ballads *are* literature, but argued that since we are dealing with a literature of tradition ballads do not benefit from being treated by standard literary analysis only. Elements of both literary criticism and anthropology must be part of the analysis, as neither of them is able to cope fully with the material.

Ólason believed that ballads are *good* literature, but was puzzled to see that ballads seem to have satisfied a need which in contemporary society is satisfied by bad literature, by the sensationalism of the yellow press. He suggested that we should take ourselves as 'source material' and ask the question: What do the ballads tell *us*?

Written response by *David Buchan*

First let me say how much I appreciate the sense of engagement brought to the subject and to his debate-role of Opponent by Mr. Pettitt. I would like to respond, in this extension of the dialogue, in the same spirit and in as succinct a fashion as possible.

Talerole Analysis and the Religious Ballads

Mr. Pettitt objects to the composition of the group of ballad-types studied: he sees it as a "selection", and selects his own preferences for inclusion and exclusion. Were, however, the researcher to set up explicit predetermined criteria and then "select", he would incur the serious danger of proceeding in a circular fashion to produce self-fulfilling results. The methodology adopted was, per contra, inductive and open. Initially there were assembled all those ballad-types labelled by critics 'religious', including those types found after Child's publication but which have had claims advanced for their being regarded as classical ballads; they were then examined to see what patterns, if any, talerole analysis would reveal. Those types which demonstrated a pronounced coherence of patterns were then seen as constituting the core of the subgenre. The eight ballad-types "chosen for study" are not "the initial selection" but in fact the final selection, where it is the internal evidence that has done the selecting. Those types mentioned by Mr. Pettitt as being in his opinion religious ballads were all analysed to see if they shared significant basic patterns: some types were found to belong predominantly to other subgenres (see below); some songs were found not to belong to the classical ballad genre at all. The two types whose status Mr. Pettitt declares without explanation to be "doubtful" prove on examination to have individual adherences to the shared basic patternings. The comments on "Sir Hugh" and "Dives and Lazarus" raise general points about the method and its application. On impressionistic grounds "Sir Hugh" could be, and has been, classed as tragic, historical, magical and marvellous, as well as religious. Given this diversity of impressionistic classifying, is it not illuminating the method should show that this type which seems to fit into many categories should not accord neatly with the patternings of the religious subgenre? With regard to "Dives and Lazarus": the proposition, in the words of the logicians, was not that all rotten apples were in the barrel but that all apples in the barrel were rotten. It matters little for the present perspective whether stories in other forms and media have the same characters as are found in classical ballads (the 'eternal triangle', for example, occurs in a wide range of forms); what does matter for generic understanding is whether a particular group of classical ballads have particular sets of characters-and-taleroles and stories-and-patternings. To suggest that the scope should have been widened to include "a miscellany of more or less religious narrative songs, both ballads and non-ballads" is to fall into the rotten apples fallacy and to ignore the given concern of the symposium and the paper - the classical ballads.

Talerole Analysis and Ballad Tradition

The central problem in communication here lies with the concept of type, which is basic to folkloristic enquiry (whether one is dealing with narrative-type or house-type or ballad-type) but which does not appear in the Opponent's analytic vocabulary. Mr. Pettitt declares that "The Wife of Usher's Well" both "is a religious ballad" and "is not a religious ballad". A certain confusion results. He is, however, talking not about 'a' ballad "The Wife of Usher's Well" but about certain versions of "The Wife of Usher's Well". Considerable confusion in argument results if one uses the phrase 'a' or 'the' ballad to refer to one text and also to refer to the entity formed by all the related texts. That is why folklorists, for clarity of thought, will use the terms 'version' to refer to an individual rendition and 'type' to refer to the essential constants that unite the versions. Given the dynamic fluidity of tradition a type's versions will naturally show variables as well as constants. These have to be taken account of in the overall perspective, but it is the constants which govern the conception of the type. Anyone acquainted with Aarne-Thompson's *Types of the Folktale* is unlikely to agree that to deal with type is to deal with "some conglomerate of conveniently selected bits and pieces". The paper is concerned with the types, that is, the essential constants, rather than the variables, just as, at one level of abstraction higher, it is concerned with the constants that among the types indicate subgenres.

Talerole analysis operates by considering certain essential constants of the type rather than the aberrant variables in a minority number of versions. "The Wife of Usher's Well" as ballad-type belongs in patternings to the Revenant Ballads subgenre (see the article forthcoming in *Western Folklore*); a minority number of versions of the type have religious elements. That does not mean the *type* should be classed as belonging to the Religious Ballads subgenre; rather, it means that those versions with religious elements should ideally, i.e., if no circumscriptions of time or space exist, be discussed in the context of the Religious subgenre. There are other types, not mentioned by Mr. Pettitt, which also have unusual versions with religious elements, and they too would have been discussed if scope had allowed. For such discussion to be useful, however, the various interactive factors need to be known. For "The Wife of Usher's Well", for example, one needs to know the basic features of the Revenant Ballads subgenre to which the type belongs and the basic features of the Religious Ballads subgenre which may have influenced certain versions, in order to see the nature of the interaction. First, clearly, there have to be established the essential characteristics of the various subgeneric groupings before the various cross-influencings and interactions can be effectively perceived. My preliminary findings indicate that (as was suggested in "Propp's Tale Role and a Ballad Repertoire") some types are hybrids, with talerole patterns amalgamating elements from two distinct sets of subgeneric groupings, and that some versions of some types are also hybrids. After the establishment of the subgeneric characteristics can come the investigation of the different hybridisations, but that is a second stage of research. During the first stage the concern lies with establishing the essential subgeneric characteristics.

For clear understanding of the type, there are two basic requirements: that the researcher knows the range of versions; and that the researcher is able to discriminate soundly between the constants and the variables in that range of versions. Mr. Pettitt in his paper disagreed with the summation of "The Maid and the Palmer" but then in discussion admitted that he knew only the English version (and Scottish fragment) but knew not the nineteenth century Scottish version or the twentieth-century Irish versions in Bronson. His dismissal of the type-summation of "The Cherry-Tree Carol", on the other hand, relies on heavily emphasis ing minor variables and downplaying the essential elements.

In sum, then, the disagreements derive from the Opponent's difficulty in accepting the folkloristic concept of type or an inductive approach, one that works from the material towards generalisations and not the other way round. Finally, let me acknowledge in welcome fashion his statements on the "practical feasibility" of talerole analysis and "the suitability of talerole configurations as a means of defining and characterizing the subgenres of balladry", and thank him for the stimulating vigour of his opposition.

Session 3

Ballad Formulas
and
the Language of Tradition

Written paper
BY FLEMMING G. ANDERSEN

i

The concept of 'continuity' is fundamental to any tradition, and it is widely acknowledged that a specific kind of poetic language has been continually employed in the telling of the short dramatic stories that we generally refer to as 'traditional ballads'. The most striking elements of the highly conventionalized ballad diction are the formulas, which are regularly used to meet recurrent narrative needs. Over the years such formulas, originally unique expressions, have lost all signs of specificity and have become typical in form and content.

Formulas are as hard to define as they are easy to recognize. Some scholars have maintained that formulas should not be singled out for specific investigation since really everything in the traditional language is formulaic.[1] The present paper, nevertheless, ventures on a formula analysis, in the belief that there is indeed some significance in extracting the most frequent, typical elements from traditional ballad diction, as they can be demonstrated to behave in particular ways. Elaborating on Milman Parry's classic definition of the formula - as well as on a few other studies - we may offer the following outline of the formulas in Anglo-Scottish traditional balladry: [2]

1. Cf. David Buchan's observation quoted in Bengt R. Jonsson, "A report on the Transactions. The Stockholm Conference on Ballad Formulas, May 24-26, 1976", Sumlen 1978, 94-101 (p. 96)
2. Cf. Milman Parry, "Studies in the Epic Technique of Oral Verse-Making: [I + II]", Harvard Studies in Classical Philology, 41 (1930), 73-147; and 43 (1932), 1-50. Michael Nagler,

Ballads are essentially *narrative* songs, and the formulas serve a distinctly narrative function, denoting recurrent significant acts. They play an important role in the scenic unfolding of ballad stories, and on the basis of identity of the narrative content (idea) they may be grouped into *formula families*. The form of the formula phrases within single families may vary greatly, but on the other hand formulas do not appear in entirely arbitrary shapes. They have been moulded into recognizable forms characterized by both linguistic innovation and preservation.

Norm-setting tradition has influenced the formulas in another way. Traditional ballad formulas possess distinctive stylistic qual ities, which may be termed 'supra narrative' in the sense that they add a dimension to the immediate narrative function of the phrases in question. The frequent employment of members of the same formula families in similar situations has imbued them with promi nent overtones, which establish specific relations between the formulas and their contexts. For instance, a formula family like SHE HAD NOT PULLED A FLOWER BUT ONE 3) will be used as forewarning of a violent act, typically that of sexual assault, and will consequently evoke specific expectations with regard to the ensuing story. It will mark a dramatic turn of events, and the act signalled by the formula will constitute the kernel conflict in the

Spontaneity and Tradition. A Study in the Oral Art of Homer, Berkeley: University of California Press, 1974. Paul Kiparsky, "Oral Poetry: Some Linguistic and Typological Considerations", in Oral Literature and the Formula, ed. by Benjamin Stolz and Richard Shannon, Ann Arbor: Center for Co-ordination of Ancient and Modern Studies, The University of Michigan, 1976, pp. 73-125. Otto Holzapfel, Studien zur Formelhaftigkeit der mittelalterlichen dänischen Volksballade, Frankfurt a.M., 1969; and Holzapfel's recent book Det balladeske. Fortællemåden i den ældre episke folkevise, Odense: Odense Universitetsforlag, 1980. For a discussion of these studies and for a full exposition of my own views on formula definition and formula functions, see my Commonplace and Creativity. The Role of Formulaic Diction in Anglo-Scottish Traditional Balladry. Odense: Odense University Press, 1985.
3.   The use of capital letters indicates the entire formula family, not a particular formula line or formula stanza.

ballad story. Formulas ensure coherence on many levels in ballad texts, paving the way for also a stylistic appreciation of the traditional ballad as a popular art form.

The ballad formulas belong to the genre as traditional narrative tools, and they are sufficiently flexible to be handled individually by the ballad singers. Denoting recurrent significant acts formulas may be viewed as the highlights in the ballad stories, but they themselves are not narrative fundamentals. They cannot be reduced to an abstract structural pattern underlying all ballad texts: they are concrete renditions of particular significant acts, and what is deemed significant has been determined by the tradition itself - not according to a specific theory of folk narratives. It is in the concrete interplay of repetition patterns, formulas and context-bound phrases that the ballads structure their dramatic narratives, not in a fixed formula sequence, but in clusters of dramatic intensity. The supra-narrative functions of character portrayal and narrative anticipation enhance the dramatic effects, the more so since the supra-narrative functions of the British formulas can be subcategorized under the two headings 'Love' and 'Death' - Love comprising such features as falling in love, the love affair, the sexual act, pregnancy and childbirth, and Death comprising all aspects of aggression, confrontation, violence, death and burial. Typically, each formula family will exploit its own supra-narrative spectrum, so even with this dense concentration around the two thematic cores there is ample room for stylistic diversification.

As illustration of some of the specific functions of formulaic diction the remaining part of the study will be devoted to a discussion of one formula family - the recurrent 'letter-reading formula' - which is used in contexts when news conveyed in a letter is made known to the principal characters, for example in the following formulation: 4)

> The first look that Johnny lookd,
> A loud laughter gae he;
> But the next look that Johnny gae,
> The tear blinded his ee.   (Child 99B 12)

With its minute close-up on the character's face the formula provides a powerful stylistic device, effectively presenting the

4.   This formula family is discussed in my Commonplace and Creativity, ch. 11 ix.

change in mood and thereby revealing the tragic nature of the message. From a narrative point of view the form of the formula stanza is well in tune with the general technique of traditional ballads, as it underlines the dramatic intensity in terms of anti- thetical structure: 'first' - 'laughter'; 'next' - 'tear'. On receiving the letter the lord seems delighted, obviously recognizing the hand or seal of the sender (many letters are 'sealed with his own hand'), or reading the conventional opening greeting, but as he reads on, the moment he senses the gist of the letter, happiness turns to grief. The externalization of the man's feelings helps us visualize the scene before us. 5)

On the supra-narrative level, too, the formula serves as a stage direction in the ballad drama. The formula marks the step in the story when the characters not yet deeply involved are thrust into the main conflict of the ballad, and it encompasses characterizing as well as presaging functions. The formula serves to portray the characters at a moment of crisis, and also points to the enactment of the basic conflict: the recipient of the letter is now called upon to take part actively in the ballad's action. Loosely reflecting the typical Love-Death dichotomy of traditional balladry the members of this formula family divide into two subgroups: one group is associated with correspondence concerning lovers or husbands and wives, with news of imposed marriage, of imprisonment and impending death. In this context of emotional attachment such news provokes the characters to act promptly, in an attempt to avert the tragic development (see Appendix). In the second sub- group the recipient is summoned by the king or some other person of authority. Generally the letter is not quite clear as concerns the

5.   This formula family is so common in traditional balladry that the gesture denoted by it has been viewed as the appropriate attitude for a ballad character to maintain when he receives a letter; cf. the comment made by Wolfgang Schmidt on the formula in the ballad of "Sir Patrick Spens" (Child No. 58):

> Beim Empfang eines Briefes vom König, der als solcher Ehre und Glück verheisst, der tatsächlich aber eine Un- glücksbotschaft enthält, müsste sich jeder gute Schau- spieler wie Sir Patrick Spens verhalten.

("Die Entwicklung der englisch-schottischen Volksballade", Anglia, 57 (1933), 1-77, 113-207 (p. 181).)

implications of the message, but the tragic overtones loom large as the characters act loyally upon the order (see Appendix).

The pure statistics of the WHEN JOHNIE LOOKED THE LETTER ON formula family are strongly indicative of its significance for the ballad tradition, and this point finds additional support in observations made by singers themselves. Asked to comment on the frequent occurrences of characters reading letters Stanley Robertson of Aberdeen - nephew of the celebrated Jeannie Robertson - remarked: 6)

> Always when they get a letter there's a laugh and then there's the tears. To me this represents the reality of what's happening. For the first time a person comes to his senses, an inner truth hits him, there's a new awakening ... [and] when they read it they are really, really touched.

Here, too, the formula is associated with specific overtones which are directed towards an interpretation of the characters' states of mind, at decisive points in the narrative.

In the overwhelming majority of cases the formula highlights the dramatic change in mood, but as is typical of formulaic diction, the actual wording may vary. Occasionally the antithetical structure is not exploited:

> When Messgrove lookt the letter on,
>   A waeful man was he;
> Sayin, Gin I'm gript wi Lord Barnard's wife,
>   Sure hanged I will be   (Child 81G 3)

but this does not seriously impair the formula status of the stanza. This is best viewed as another instance of formula flexibility. When the characters have distinct premonitions of what is to come there is less reason to smile. Ballad singers do not use formulas 'mechanically', and the ear- and eye-catching dichotomous structure is no strait-jacket for them. On the contrary, singers generally seem to be very consistent in their use of formulas, introducing the appropriate modifications according to particular contexts. Mrs Brown of Falkland is a case in point: in her first version of "Bonny

6.   Private tape, 1981.

Baby Livingston" (Child 222Ab), from 1800, she has the hero read
the letter concerning the imprisonment of his true-love in this
manner:

> Whan Johnie lookit the letter on,
>   A hearty laugh leuch he;
> But ere he read it till an end
>   The tear blinded his ee.   (Child 222Ab 24)

But in the version sent to Robert Jamieson a month later Mrs
Brown changed this formula stanza to describe Johnie's anger only,
in consequence of the preceding stanza (which is not in Mrs Brown's
first version - one of the few discrepancies between the two texts)
where the little messenger boy reveals the gist of the tragic news:

> 'O here's a letter I have brought,
>   Which ye maun quickly read,
> And, gin ye woud your lady save,
>   Gang back wi me wi speed.'
>
> O when he had the letter read,
>   An angry man was he;
> He says, Glenlion, thou shalt rue
>   This deed of villany!   (Child 222Aa 26-27)

The evidence is insufficient for us to draw definitive conclusions,
but it appears that singers are acutely aware of the potentialities
of formulaic diction. Surveying Mrs Brown's repertoire one is led to
believe that she deliberately chose specific formulations to go with
particular ballads, occasionally also, as in this case, with different
versions of the same ballad.7) Formulaic diction is one of the

7. Mrs Brown is particularly free in her exploitation of the
    WHERE WILL I GET A BONNY BOY formula (Child 65A
    18-21, 90A 2-3, 91C 6, 99A 7-10, 222Aa 21-24, 222Ab 21-23),
    HE'S TAEN HER BY THE MILKWHITE HAND (Child 10B 8+10,
    42A 6, 53A 19+23, C 31, 76E 8, 102A 15, 222A 6, 252C 34), and
    SHE HADNA BEEN IN FAIR ENGLAND (Child 53C 2+12, 76D
    7, 92A 9, 99A 2, 101A 2). With the WHEN BELLS WERE RUNG
    AND MASS WAS SUNG, on the other hand, she tends to

points where she can display her 're-creative' powers, in the sense
of a conscious amendment of a basically memorized text. 8)
    While Mrs Brown of Falkland is the earliest known oral source
for British balladry the earliest extensive corpus from local oral
tradition was procured by William Motherwell, who visited the
village of Kilbarchan, near Glasgow, on several occasions in 1825
and 1826, in quest of old ballads and tunes. In this relatively highly
industrialized area - Kilbarchan was one of the strongholds of the
weaving industries - he came across a number of ladies who had in
their memories a large stock of traditional ballads. It is a useful
reminder of the multifarious nature of traditional balladry that this
early material from oral tradition was recorded in an industrial
village of apparently widespread literacy. The illiterate, agricultural community envisaged by many scholars as the prerequisite of
traditional balladry is left far behind (if ever it did exist in its

employ very similar expressions, presumably because this
formula family has a particular status in her repertoire. She
uses it in one third of her ballads, obviously in consequence of
its strong overtones of sexual intercourse. By employing the
formula the 'polite' Mrs Brown can rely on the supra-narrative
function to suggest the narrative action without being explicit
(cf. Child 5A 27-28, 32 st. 18, 62E 13, 63B 21, 76E 17, 89A 5,
96A 21, 97A 8, 101A 13-14, 102A 10, (155A 10)).

8. For varying assessments of Mrs Brown, see e.g. Bertrand H.
Bronson, "Mrs Brown and the Ballad", California Folklore
Quarterly, 4 (1945), 129-40. David Fowler, A Literary History
of the Popular Ballad, Durham, N.C.: Duke University Press,
1968, ch. 10. David Buchan, The Ballad and the Folk, London:
Routledge & Kegan Paul, 1972, Part II; and Buchan's recent
article "Propp's Tale Role and a Ballad Repertoire", Journal of
American Folklore, 95 (1982), 159- 72. Holger O. Nygard, "Mrs
Brown's Recollected Ballads", in Ballads and Ballad Research,
ed. by Patricia Conroy, Seattle: University of Washington, 1978,
pp. 68-87. Flemming G. Andersen and Thomas Pettitt, "Mrs
Brown of Falkland: A Singer of Tales?", Journal of American
Folklore, 92 (1979), 1-24; and Thomas Pettitt, "Mrs Brown's
'Lass of Roch Royal' and the Golden Age of Scottish Balladry",
Jahrbuch für Volksliedforschung, 29 (1984), 13-31.

'purest' form).9) And rather than reaching for the unattainable we should be grateful for what has been preserved: in neither form nor content can the Kilbarchan material be distinguished from what is generally understood by 'traditional balladry', and it is quite evident that William Motherwell as well as the singers themselves did conceive of these ballads as traditional, both in the sense that they were frequently recorded as having lived in family tradition, and in the sense that the singers can be demonstrated to have made traditional use of formulaic diction. 10)

Three Kilbarchan singers employ the letter-reading formula family; Agnes Lyle, Mrs Thomson and Agnes Laird:11) Agnes Lyle

9.   Indeed, ballads have tended to disappoint scholars and collec-
     tors. The ballad tradition has refused to expire despite re-
     peated allegations by collectors that they were gleaning the
     last remnants of a moribund tradition.

10. Studies of the 'personal use' of formulas have stressed the
     singer's adherence to static expressions of recurrent ideas (cf.
     Wolfhart Anders, Balladensänger und mündliche Komposition.
     Untersuchungen zur englischen Traditionsballade, München:
     Wilhelm Fink Verlag, 1974), while diversified diction within a
     repertoire tends to be interpreted as 'parts of the song'
     determined by the texts themselves, cf. Kenneth A. Thigpen,
     "A Reconsideration of the Commonplace Phrase and Common-
     place Theme in the Child Ballads", Southern Folklore Quarter-
     ly, 37 (1973), 385-408. Otto Holzapfel's brief discussion of the
     formulas of Frands Povlsen is a noteworthy exception ("Skan-
     dinavische Volksballadenformeln: Merkmal traditioneller Im-
     provisation oder literarischer/verbaler Tradierung?", Sumlen
     1978, 102-121 (pp. 115-119)).

11. The ballads have been recorded in Motherwell's Manuscript and
     Notebook. For analyses of the ballads from the Kilbarchan
     area, see Thigpen, "A Reconsideration of the Commonplace
     Phrase and Commonplace Theme in the Child Ballads",and
     William McCarthy, Creativity, Tradition, and History: The
     Ballad Repertoire of Agnes Lyle of Kilbarchan, Indiana Uni-
     versity, 1978. Some of the texts recorded have been printed in
     Child's collection, and in Cuthbert P. Lyle's edition of Poems
     and Ballads from Kilbarchan, I+II, Glasgow: W. & R. Holmes,
     1929-31.

in "Sir Patrick Spens" (Child 58E 4), "Johnie Scot" (99G 5), "Lord
Derwentwater" (208A 3) and "Geordie" (209F 6); Mrs Thomson in
"Johnie Scot" (99C 6) and "Katharine Jaffray" (221J 7); and Agnes
Laird in "Johnie Scot" (99F 6). Most of the formulas are preceded
by stanzas relating the writing and sealing of the letter, which
apart from the last lines are very similar indeed (see 58E 3, 99G 4,
208A 1, 99C 5, 221J 6, 99F 5), while the formula stanzas display
significant variations:

Agnes Lyle:

> When Young Patrick read the letter lang,
>   The tear blindit his ee;
> Says Wha is this, or wha is that,
>   That's tauld the king of me?
> Altho he had been better than what he is,
>   He micht hae askt leave of me.   (Child 58E 4)

> When Johnie read this letter long,
>   The tear blindit his ee:
> 'I must away to Old England;
>   King Edward writes for me.'   (Child 99G 5)

> The very first line that my lord did read,
>   He gave a smirkling smile;
> Before he had the half o't read,
>   The tears from his eyes did fall.   (Child 208A 3)

> When she read the first of it,
>   She was baith glad and cheery;
> But before she had the half o't read,
>   She was baith sad and sorry.   (Child 209F 6)

Mrs Thomson:

> The first line of the letter he read,
>   His heart was full of joy;
> But he had not read a line past two
>   Till the salt tears blind his eye.   (Child 99C 6)

> *The first line o the letter he read,*
> *He was baith glad and fain;*
> *But or he read the letter owre*
> *He was baith pale and wan.*   *(Child 221J 7)*

Agnes Laird:

> *The first lang line that he looked to,*
> *He laughed at the same;*
> *The neist lang line that he did read,*
> *The tears did blin his een.*   *(Child 99F 6)*

What we see here is of course not free variation, but 'traditional variation' within a time-honoured framework: most of the phrases express the character's change in mood, but none of the formula stanzas are exact duplicates of each other - only two single lines suggest interdependence within their respective repertoires: 208A 3.3 and 209F 6.3 from Agnes Lyle, and 99C 6.1 and 221J 7.1 from Mrs Thomson. Reading the first part of the letters the characters laugh/give a smile/are glad and cheery, but before they have read the letter/half of it/the next line tears fall from their eyes/blind their eyes, and they are pale and wan/sad and sorry. The two one-mood variants from Agnes Lyle's repertoire, on the other hand, are virtually identical: when he reads the 'long' letter the tears blind his eyes. But in no case do the above actualizations of the formula family appear to be dependent on the wordings in other versions of the same ballads, nor indeed from other ballads.12) The diversified picture seems to reflect active participation on the parts of the singers themselves, who have deliberately introduced or retained these formulations.

The approximation towards static expression in the one-mood

12. Only single lines have occasional parallels:
    "Before he had the half o't read": cf. Child 99A 18.3, 99H 13.3, 99Q 10.3.
    "The first line of the letter he read": cf. Child 208 2.1.
    "The first long line he looked to": cf. Child 58J 4.1, 66A 14.1, 99E 6.1, 208E 3.1, 208G 2.1, 208H 2.1, 209G 2.1, 238B 10.1.
    "The next line that he read": cf. Child 58A 4.3, 58C 4.3, 238G 7.2, 238I 4.3.

variants is determined by the supra-narrative function of these stanzas. Both instances concern letters from a king summoning the hero to come to the court, either to perform a dangerous task (as in "Sir Patrick Spens" (58E)) or for a personal confrontation with the king over his daughter (as in "Johnie Scot" (99G)). Agnes Lyle's third instance, from "Lord Derwentwater" (208A) also concerns a letter from the king, and this time the hero is summoned to the court to be hanged for treason.13) In this case the wording seems to be somewhat influenced by the ballad story itself, i.e., context-bound: all versions have a combination of the terms 'smile' and 'tears'. But Agnes Lyle has left her distinctive mark upon the formula: hers is the only version to introduce the modifier 'smirkling', which lends an unequivocally ominous tone to the expression, in line with her other renditions. In "Geordie" (209F), on the other hand, the initial joy comes to prevail: the lady is informed of the impending death of her imprisoned husband, but acting resolutely she manages to have him freed.

Mrs Thomson and Agnes Laird produce only two-mood variants, and in all three cases the letter is sent by a damsel in distress to her lover. In "Johnie Scot" (99C + F) the princess sends word of her imprisonment, and in "Katharine Jaffray" (221J) the girl informs her lover that she is forced to marry someone else. In both cases the conflict is happily resolved, and the true-lovers are reunited. While Mrs Thomson and Agnes Laird, then, stress the emotional aspects of the love relationship with their letter-reading formula in "Johnie Scot", Agnes Lyle treats the ballad as basically a story of personal confrontation between Johnie and the king - as her renditions of other formulas in that ballad bear additional witness to.14) Also Mrs Thomson and Agnes Laird use formulaic diction distinctively. It is characteristic that Mrs Thomson should have the

13. As William McCarthy observes, Agnes Lyle employs the "King's Letter Theme" three times, and in each case "perfidy seems afoot" (Creativity, Tradition and History, pp. 55-56).
14. Cf. the three singers' use of WORD'S GANE UP AND WORD'S GANE DOON (Child 99C 2, 99F 1-2), THE FIRST TOWN THAT THEY CAME TO (99C 11, 99G 9-10), WHEN HE CAME TO FAIR ELLEN'S GATES (99C 12+15, 99F 10, 99G 11), and SHE LOOKIT OVER HER FATHER'S CASTLE WA' (99C 12, 99G 11).

letter sent by the princess's "own boy at command" (99C 5.4). She
is very fond of the WHERE WILL I GET A BONNY BOY formula,
and frequently expresses her explicit concern for the little messenger boy (cf. Child 65E 21.3-4, 83E 34.3-4). Agnes Laird, too, is
aware of the supra-narrative function of that formula family (and
uniquely states it in her version of "Prince Robert" (Child 87C
12.3-4)), just as she realizes the significance of the present
letter-reading formula. Quite appropriately she *omits* it in her
version of "The Gay Goshawk", since the supra-narrative potential
would be out of place here: the girl receives a letter asking her to
come to her true-love, and she has a plan ready immediately.
Feigning death she knows that she will be 'buried' in Scotland, to be
reunited with her lover:

> *She has taken the letter up,*
> *And read it speedilie:*
> *'O mother, the queen, O mother, the queen,*
> *Grant this request to me;*
> *Whenever I do chance for to die,*
> *In Scotland gar bury me.'*   *(Child 96D 6)*

This stanza has none of the formulaic paraphernalia.

In traditional form the formulas are potent narrative tools for
the singers, and the present formula family provides some evidence
as to how it came to acquire its traditional shape and function. In
the ballad of "Tom Potts", in all versions, we come across a very
circumstantial account of a similar piece of narrative: a young girl
wants to send a letter to her poor true-love, informing him that
she has been forced to marry a rich man. The little messenger boy
is instructed to watch the lover carefully as he reads the letter, in
order to interpret his reaction rightly: "Looke thou marke his
contenance well" (Child 109A 15.1, cf. B 16.1 and C 9.4). For if he
smiles, she must seek another true-love, but if he blushes "in his
heart he will sorry be" (B 18.2), and she will remain faithful to him.
As he reads the letter, then, he sheds tears (A 20, B 21, C 15), and
everything eventually turns out all right.

All versions of the ballad were recorded in the middle of the
seventeenth century, thus predating most of the proper formulas of
this family, and from the point of view of relative chronology we

may say that we here see the forerunner of the formula.15) The stanzas are explicitly associated with personal characterization: the boy is asked to *interpret* the man's emotional response as he receives the message. Genuine formulas do not guide the audience in this overt manner. In tradition character portrayal and presaging function gradually became implicit in this formula family. The hypothesis that proper ballad formulas are the eventual marriage between act denoted and act interpreted, in one expression pregnant with supra-narrative function will at least help explain occurrences of this kind (and indeed other early near-formulaic expressions related to other families). 16)

Discussing the letter-reading formula in the Kilbarchan material Kenneth A. Thigpen concludes that

> It should be clear from these examples that the words of the song itself, manifested by appearance in two or more unrelated texts, can be more influential in causing the usage of similar stanzas for similar themes in different ballads sung by a single informant than reliance on static expression of similar thematic conceptualizations. 17)

i.e., formulas different in form have been determined by the ballad stories (they are 'parts of the song'), while only static expressions are 'personal formulas'. In view of the above discussion I would argue rather that formulas belong to the entire genre and they may be employed more or less individually by different types of singers. There really is a continuum of formulaic flexibility, not merely instances of idiosyncratic formulations determined by the ballads, and more or less static expressions such as 'personal formulas'. Ballad singers use formulaic language much more freely, and their 'traditional re-creativity' comes out in the *degree* to which they exploit the potentialities (narrative and supra-narrative) of that

15. Roughly contemporary instances are Child 271A 85, 271B 53 and 169B 5, and they too are somewhat special.
16. Cf. e.g. HE FELL LOW DOWN ON HIS KNEE, HE LOOKED OVER HIS LEFT SHOULDER and HE'S TAEN HER BY THE MILKWHITE HAND, which are discussed in my Commonplace and Creativity.
17. "A Reconsideration of the Commonplace Phrase and Commonplace Theme in the Child Ballads", p. 393.

diction. Formula analysis along the lines suggested here shows that formulas are an important vehicle for that gradual re-interpretation and re-shaping which is so vital for the life and survival of the ballad tradition.

Odense University

APPENDIX

Subgroup 1:

"Willie's Lyke Wake" (Child 25E 5)
"Lord Ingram and Chiel Wyet" (Child 66A 14)
"Johnie Scot" (Child 99A 18, B 12, C 6, D 9, E 6, F 6, H 13, I 7, K 7,
        N 19, Q 10; Bronson 99.6 st. 19)
"Geordie" (Child 209A 3, B 5, D 7, F 6, G 2, H 5, I 7; Bronson 209.3
        st. 10, 4 st. 10, 34 st. 7)
"Katharine Jaffray" (Child 221J 7; Crawfurd 66 st. 2; Bronson 221.6
        st. 3, 11 st. 4)
"Bonny Baby Livingston" (Child 222Aa 27, Ab 24, D 8, App. V
        st. 17)
"Andrew Lammie" (Child 233A 24; Stanley Robertson st. 14, 1981)
"The Earl of Aboyne" (Child 235 App. V st. 14)
"Glenlogie" (Child 238A 15, B 10, F 8, G 7, I 4; Bronson 238.10 st.
        8, 12 st. 9; Stanley Robertson st. 8, 1981)
"The Rantin Laddie" (Child 240A 7, B 7, C 18, D 8; Bronson 240.3
        st. 13)
"Lang Johnny More" (Bronson 251.5 st. 20)

Subgroup 2;

"Sir Patrick Spens" (Child 58A 4, B 4, C 4, E 4, H 5, I 5, J 4)
"Little Musgrave and Lady Barnard" (Child 81G 3)
"Brown Adam" (Child 98C 10)
"Johnie Scot" (Child 99G 5, L 5)
"Johnie Armstrong" (Child 169B 5)
"Lord Derwentwater" (Child 208A 3, B 2, C 3, D 2, E 3, F 3, G 2,
        H 2, I 3, J 2; Crawfurd 3 st. 2; Bronson 208.3 st. 2)
"Redesdale and Wise William" (Child 246A 8, B 6)
"Lord William" (Child 254B 5)
"Fair Rosanne" (Crawfurd 18 st. 8)

Bronson = Bertrand H. Bronson, ed. *The Traditional Tunes of the
        Child Ballads.* 4 vols. Princeton: Princeton University Press,
        1959-72.

Child = Francis J. Child, ed. *The English and Scottish Popular Ballads*. 1882-98, rpt. in 5 vols. New York: Dover Publications, 1965.

Crawfurd = Emily Lyle, ed. *Andrew Crawfurd's Collection of Ballads and Songs*. Edinburgh: The Scottish Text Society, 1975.

Oral presentation by *Flemming G. Andersen*

In this oral presentation of my paper "Ballad Formulas and the Language of Tradition" I shall offer a survey of the main points, as well as outline the assumptions behind the formula analysis, and point to some of the implications of the approach taken here.

Some fundamental issues concerning this type of analysis were discussed this morning in connection with Reimund Kvideland's paper, which advocates the priority of investigations into social behaviour over the 'traditional' text-oriented studies of specific genres. This kind of debate has been going on for a while, and although the time may not yet be ripe for a full reconciliation or compromise between the two sides I will suggest that studies of textual structures (sometimes known as 'skeleton studies') may after all provide some of the answers that the students of 'song activity' - the singing activists - are looking for.

Kvideland characterized tradition as a process (p. 15), and this is one of the assumptions also underlying the formula analysis, but, like David Buchan (p. 27) I view this process diachronically, stressing the aspect of 'continuity'. In a diachronic perspective, in which we include the old tradition, we must take as our point of departure that which has been preserved - and most often this will be the texts. But then of course we must work our way outwards from the text, and try to establish as much as we can about the historical, social and cultural context. For with this kind of ballad tradition, not until we know what, how and when people were singing can we really ask, *why* did they sing. This paper is an attempt to describe *how* ballads were sung - and indeed *are* sung - for with the Anglo-Scottish tradition we are fortunate enough to be dealing with a living ballad tradition. And we must take that entire tradition, old and modern, into account.

A basic problem in this context of formula studies is the characterization of the ballad formula. What does it look like, and where do we look for it? Formulas - which are traditional in the sense that they have been used and changed continually over many years - are far easier to spot than they are to define. Like ballads themselves they are awkward things, but what we can say is that 1. they are multiform units: that is, a formula will hardly ever appear in exactly the same form twice. 2. Formulas express significant

UNIVERSITY OF WINCHESTER
LIBRARY

narrative ideas, and 3. they are imbued with certain stylistic overtones, the supra-narrative qualities. 4. Finally, we may divide formulas into specific groups, formula families, if they, in similar form, express the same narrative idea. The question of where to find the ballad formulas is a complex one, as well. As Kvideland disapprovingly points out in his paper (p. 13) genre-oriented scholarship is usually concerned with the concepts of 'orality, rurality, anonymity, continuity'. And while I will still maintain that 'continuity' is an essential term, I find the other concepts less useful - like Kvideland - as characterizations of the contexts of the ballads that contain formulaic diction. Formulas are not typical of ballads in oral tradition only - 'oral' here simply meaning 'transmitted by word of mouth'. They are also found in the written tradition, that is, in texts on broadsheets. Formulas *can* be characteristic of the ballads in an agricultural community, but they may be equally typical of the ballads that were recorded in an industrialized area, such as the ballads of Kilbarchan, Renfrewshire, which I have looked at in my paper. Ballads are oral *and* written, they are found in rural *and* industrial contexts, they are old *and* new - still alive to-day, most emphatically among the travellers in Scotland. Balladry is a composite of many elements, and we want our concept of tradition to take all these aspects into account. So quite obviously we cannot take Child's edition of *The English and Scottish Popular Ballads* as *the* ballad canon. Traditional balladry is found also outside this standard edition, both in earlier and later collections, and indeed many texts included in Child's collection can hardly be termed 'traditional ballads'. Ballads are a narrative mode, not a closed literary category with its own one authoritative edition.

A final problem in this connection is the relationship between 'formula' and 'ballad'. It is evident that formulaic diction is part and parcel of the ballad's narrative technique: the traditional ballad is characterized by the dramatic interplay of formulas, context-bound phrases and verbal patternings. But we must allow for the peculiar nature of ballads. The eventual characterization of a text as a 'traditional ballad' is essentially the exercise of determining the *degree* to which it conforms to the balladic narrative technique: there are no steadfast, objective criteria. This is also true, on a different level, of the formulas. Formulaic phraseology may swing between the questionably formulaic and the emphatically formulaic, and exactly when the pendulum reaches the indisputably formulaic balladic narrative technique is a very delicate matter. There is no given percentage of formulaicness, even if we were desperate enough to try to figure it out, which invariably stamps a text as balladic.

What, then, are the advantages of a formula analysis, if any? And here I will have to claim that there are some. For one thing, as just mentioned, the formula analysis will have some bearing on the generic question - intriguing and vexing as it may be. But what is more important, the characterization of the ballad formulas as multiform units with specific supra-narrative qualities will pave the way for an investigation into the ballads as *popular art form*. Owing to their formal flexibilities formulas may be handled individually by the singers, who may introduce minor variations - or retain specific formulations - in order to produce what they regard as their 'own' versions of the ballads. And on the supra-narrative level singers may exploit the stylistic overtones, by playing the formulas off against each other to generate 'new' clusters of dramatic intensity in their ballads.

I have looked at one ballad formula in particular   the letter reading formula, which illustrates most of the points concerning formulaic diction in general, and which is found in for instance this shape:

> *The first look that Johnny lookd,*
> *A loud laughter gae he;*
> *But the next look that Johnny gae*
> *The tear blinded his ee.*

In my paper I have tried to demonstrate 1. the formal variability and 2. the supra-narrative stability of the formula family, by drawing attention to the characterizing and the presaging function: the formula portrays the characters at moments of crisis, and points to the enactment of the central conflict.

On the basis of the general picture that emerges from a consideration of all the occurrences of this one formula family I then take a closer look at three singers from one area to see how they, as individuals, exploit this particular formula. While oral and written traditions alike provide the material for the overall survey of formulaic diction, only a consideration of identified singers can tell us something about the individual handling of the ballad tradition. And we observe two things: we see that singers use distinct formulations; and we see that they use formulas consistently. The two subgroups of supra-narrative overtones are employed discriminatingly to produce different effects - in one and the same ballad, the story of "Johnie Scot". The singers clearly have distinct ways of narrating that story, in terms of 'traditional variation' within a certain framework.

The story of "Johnie Scot" is that of an unacceptable liaison between the Scottish Johnie and the English princess, that is, unacceptable to the girl's parents. They place their daughter in confinement, and having been informed of his true-love's imprisonment Johnie summons a group of men to go against the English king. And in a duel against one of the king's men Johnie 'wins' the princess. The letter-formula is employed by all three singers: Mrs Thomson and Agnes Laird use the two-mood variants (first Johnie smiles, and then he weeps) in connection with the letter from the girl, which informs Johnie of her distress. By employing these particular variants Mrs Thomson and Agnes Laird emphasize the emotional attachment between the two lovers, and indeed their versions tend to stress emotional relationships, as evidenced by their employment of other formulas - for instance they both open with a rumour-formula disclosing the girl's pregnancy, and the outcome of the formula is an inevitable strain on any parent-daughter relationship. In Agnes Lyle's version, on the other hand, we come across a one-mood variant of the letter-reading formula (in this case the letter was sent by the king himself) and the conflict in this version is fundamentally one of personal confrontation between the king and his subject - as is also indicated by Lyle's use of other formulas, which have the function of pointing to violent confrontation between opponents.

In Agnes Lyle's version, then, Johnie is primarily fighting *against* the English king (and he brags of his victory), but in the other versions Johnie is primarily fighting *for* his true-love. Towards the end of the story   rs Thomson introduces some formulas which disturb the picture of the eventually happy marriage between the two lovers, while Agnes Laird has her formulaic overtones operate on the emotional level throughout, ending of a note of unstained happiness, so that we have three distinct renditions of the ballad in this one area.

Singers, then, appear to be acutely aware of the potentials of formulaic diction. With the old tradition this assessment can only be based on interpretation, and then only in connection with analyses of full ballad repertoires. Here again, of course, the situation is far from ideal. We can never be certain that the entire repertoire of a singer has been preserved - collectors may have left out items for any number of reasons. But imperfect as it is the old ballad material does provide some remarkable instances of formulaic awareness.

The celebrated Mrs Brown of Falkland is a case in point. In my paper (p. 60) I have described one of her renditions of the BONNY BOY formula - and with this formula family she never resorts to the same formulation. This is true also of her use of another formula; the formula relating how someone takes a person by the milkwhite hand - a well-known formula family which she for instance employs in the ballad of "The Two Sisters" (Child 10):

Two sisters are being courted by the same man, whom they both love. The courting squire decides in favour of the younger girl, who is then drowned by her jealous sister. The body is later recovered, and musicians passing by the body take parts of it to make an instrument out of them. And this instrument reveals the murder and demands revenge on the cruel sister. This story is very popular in the Anglo-Scottish tradition - as elsewhere - old and modern. All versions agree on the central act, the drowning of the sister, but Mrs Brown's is the only version to anticipate this dramatic event by a formula: 'she's taken her by the milkwhite hand/and led her down to yon sea strand', which is known from a number of other contexts; contexts of prediction of murder and rape. By using it here Mrs Brown accentuates the love-death theme, weaves the narrative more tightly together, evoking associations of murdered sweethearts and sexual assault, adding a dimension to this particular ballad story.

But these are isolated instances, and you may still ask whether the concept of formula is not a figment of the ballad scholar's imagination. I don't believe so. For we do have access to authoritative statements on this matter - from the singers themselves. The modern tradition is of invaluable help here, and we must welcome the opportunity of being able to ask the singers the kinds of questions we would have liked the old collectors to have asked. Naturally we cannot tell them: please list the narrative and supra-narrative functions of formulaic diction in your ballads, but

we can ask them to comment on some of the repeated phrases: why
is it that some people cry when they receive a letter, or why do
they look over their left shoulders. I have tried to obtain this kind
of information from some of the travellers in Scotland, and, as
always, the singers are very obliging and willing to talk about their
tradition. One of the most extensive repertoires in the modern
tradition is that of Stanley Robertson - nephew of the well-known
singer Jeannie Robertson - and he has offered some pertinent
observations, for instance on the letter-reading formula (which I
quote on p. 59), in which he stresses what might be termed the
characterizing function of that formula. He also notes the associations of another formula; the formula relating the look over one's
left shoulder:

> When a person has something in his mind that he feels is so
> very obvious, he can imagine that people can read his
> thoughts. So if a person is trying to hide his eyes, or turning
> round to look, it usually means that there could be an act of
> deception, a change of circumstance, such things as a plot
> for revenge, a plan for an elopement, a woman going to run
> away from her sweetheart or her husband.
>   (Adapted from private tape, 1981).

It is quite evident, then, that the singers are aware of these
phrases, that they attach particular importance to them, and that
they are susceptible to their specific stylistic qualities. The singers
recognize these formulas as something special, just as - I believe -
they recognize ballads as a peculiar specimen of folk song. They
have a clear notion of 'big ballads', 'classical ballads', etc.

It is concrete evidence of this kind, coupled with the textual
analyses, which helps us understand how singers conceive of the
narrative technique, and understand how they handle the tradition.
Formulaic diction constitutes a specialized language, created in
tradition. It is concerned with presenting narrative information in a
dramatic manner, and with translating human experience into an
artistic medium. This typically involves the interplay of aspects of
LOVE and ᴅEATH, which are so immediatly appealing to the
singers. And this relationship between singers and their ballads is
also a topic of formula studies. So also for skeleton scholars,
formula freaks (or whatever you may want to call us) the ultimate

concern is with the singers, with the interaction of narrative mode
and content, with the context in which ballads have been used, and
are used.

Opposition by *Otto Holzapfel*

Reimund Kvideland focussed on social behaviour or singing activity
to bring us on the way to put new questions to our material or to
put the right questions to the right material. I found the statement
useful; even the remark that we know little or nothing about
context in connection with the so-called medieval ballad is necessary. Moreover, Reimund Kvideland's contribution questioned the
notion of the ballad as 'literature'. As Vésteinn Ólason pointed out,
we are concerned with folkloristic material. With David Buchan's
paper we began a discussion of type and genre. Tradition is not only
what was handed over, but what is going on at the moment of
singing, we learned from Reiund Kvideland. Tradition is what is
sung in a ballad, David Buchan told us. Now we try to take a
further step: not *why* or *what* but *how* something is told in a ballad,
and here we have the question of formula. Let me say, that the
notion of singing activity helps us to understand and to describe
something we have tended to neglect in the past. In the same way
the notion of type and genre helps us to describe something we
need to understand. Let us bring the label 'formula' into the
discussion now. We have to consider the facts themselves, and then
subsequently determine whether we used the right terms or not.

I am very grateful to be allowed to comment on Flemming G.
Andersen's paper. I basically agree with his manner of formula
analysis. As there is no need to repeat his arguments I shall start *in
medias res* and take up those points which still seem problematic to
me, and I am sure more will turn up in the discussion following. I
know his paper is part of a greater project already finished, and I
hope my questions are not merely due to misunderstanding or
shortening of arguments. Let us start with the formula itself which
here is understood as the opposite of individual wording. I do not
discuss the very analysis of the chosen formula, the "looked the
letter on formula". This analysis seems clear and concise to me and
I fully agree with the results.

But with the documentation presented there is little evidence
of the evolution from "originally unique expression" (p. 55) over
"forerunner of the formula" (p. 67) to 'ballad formula'. It does not
seem helpful to fill in the missing arguments with facts from
relative or real chronology (there are some 17th century texts

mentioned, p. 66). The ballad at its highest point of development fits only into an ideal form of the folk ballad, called ballad type or in Max Lüthi's diction 'Zielform'. Formulaic diction differs more according to its proximity to or distance from an ideal ballad form than according to its historical development. Material in folk tradition defies the classic philological model of a 'Stemma' with older roots and younger leaves. A 20th century version may in this sense be more archaic than a 15th century manuscript. If the ballad diction, and I agree, is characterized by the use of formulas, these elements have to be argued as parts of a ballad definition. The forerunner may be on the level of an individual poetry as a model for a ballad. The folk ballad itself is *per se* formulaic.

In this respect a singer uses a formula within the given frame of a formula family, as Andersen states, or he does not use it, i.e., he employs a variation or an individual wording. A singer is to be recognized as more or less traditional in such a process. He is, and I agree, in his singing characterized by both "innovation and preservation" (p. 56). Innovation seems only to be possible on the basis of a generally accepted typical ballad language, of, as Andersen says, a "highly conventionalized ballad diction" (p. 55), and I agree.

If a singer is less traditional, he does not stick to the "continuity" (p. 55) – but, and here I see a basic problem of his paper not yet solved, formulaic diction is maintained even within a 'discontinuity' of tradition. Formulaic diction is easier to recognize where this dis-continuity is a fact. A 'dying tradition' or the maintenance of a *status quo ante* clearly gives the herring-bone of ballad formulas, whereas in a continuity of living tradition innovation may conceal these elements. (The term 'dying tradition' here has nothing to do with the dubious concept of organic development from roots to leaves of the 'ballad tree', but has to do with the fact that a lot of ballad texts have been recorded from a failing memory about something gone away, not from a performance at present.) And naturally I do not understand dis-continuity as absence of ballad singing at all, but as a lack of acquired knowledge about ballad style and content. This lack of 'education' in ballad singing is, I believe, the normal status of an unskilled singer, of the – as it were – everyday-user of the song. The traditor himself is often an outstanding person in a small society. Should we say: there are singers who sing, there are people who listen and join in the singing on the one hand, and there is 'the' singer who also carries on and keeps up the singing activity in an expansive way. He is concerned with active, performed tradition, but he needs the basis of acceptance.

It is a fact that singers, and especially those who in my opinion are highly 'traditional', do maintain a formulaic diction which even seems to be senseless, contradictory or non-sense in context. Innovation, not only variation by faults or mishearings, must be a sign of a certain understanding of the ballad as a genre, but the key to the tradition must be rigid and non-individual preservation. In my opinion these problems are only to be discussed within a repertory analysis of the single singer, and in most cases we do not have the material for such an analysis.

What we do study in the given corpus of our standard ballad editions is the framework of conventionalized ballad diction, of preservation, of - may I use this contradictory term - 'discontinuity in tradition'. Every living process of singing activity means innovation and means a step away from convention. Convention means formula use, and formulaic ballad diction is to be observed most clearly in the 'frozen' situation of dis-continuity, of so-called dying tradition, with its lack of knowledge about the ballad as a genre. Here I do not use dis-continuity in the same sense as Reimund Kvideland. I understand continuity as communication, as a process, dis-continuity as immobility, the 'foot dragging' of transmission. In this way 'continuity' is not the only concept for tradition, so is dis-continuity. In most cases, highly formulaic ballad texts have not been recorded from a skilled singer, but are the frozen documents of a dying tradition. This is my hypothesis. When Flemming G. Andersen speaks about a singer, he may mean only a skilled singer. Most performances we have are not like this. This is for instance obvious in the Danish ballad documentation of Evald Tang Kristensen in the late 19th century (cf. my article in *Sumlen* 1978, especially p. 115 f).

So do we really dare to say - again in a seeming contradiction, but in any case again to play the *advocatus diaboli* for the ensuing discussion - that "traditional ballad formulas possess distinctive stylistic qualities" (p. 56)? Yes, I agree, but this is a question of ballad aesthetics. So I relate the term 'tradition' to an 'artistic communication' - Reimund Kvideland mentioned it. Here, and I hope to agree, I see some identity between Andersen's "ballad formulas" and what I call "epic formulas". We are obviously on the other side of what until now has been characterized as 'empty formulas', 'fillers' or 'mere repetition'. (And also beyond Lord's concept of a "quantity analysis" of formulaic diction.)

Like Flemming G. Andersen I recognize epic formulaic ballad diction as meaningful and even significant convention. It is true that every expression has its development, history and background, but the typical ballad-like expression is in my opinion a 'target form' (German 'Zielform') to which preservation tends to get closer, while innovation tends to move away from it. That is to say, there is no existing 'ideal ballad', but documents which taken as a whole corpus reveal the trend of the genre. Discussion of ballad formulas is at the very core of the discussion of the ballad genre.

But here we have more or less a contra-position to the question of repertory analysis of an individual singer. In my opinion the discussion has to go on in these two directions: genre analysis in a corpus of widespread collections and analyses of individual repertories. Mixing the two will remain unsatisfactory.

Concerning the "narrative fundamentals" (p. 57) I agree with the opposition of 'love' and 'death' as a tool for structure analysis, but to reveal the narrative and supra-narrative function of this fundamental constellation within a genre as the ballad or in relation to the so-called 'world-view' of an individual singer would mean investigating clearly distinct areas. As I said, we should not pose the wrong question to the given material, but we should look for adequate material to our changing questions. I come to the end: the problem was not solved by transferring Lord's ideas (I say Lord, not Parry) to ballad material, nor will the problem be solved by examining repertoires in Child or most other ballad editions. Here I see what Flemming G. Andersen quotes as a "private tape" (p. 59) as a step in the right direction. We need more observations of singing practice, and I hope he can carry this work on.

Discussion. Notes by *Thomas Pettitt*

Replying, Flemming G. Andersen discussed the question of the forerunners of the formu'as, raised by Holzapfel. He had not set out to discover these in collecting his material, where the criteria for selection had been formulas where the supra-narrative element was intrinsic to the formula itself, this being the main topic of his investigation. He had however encountered some instances where the supra-narrative function was performed by explicit verbal interpretation of what was happening in the story, and it is doubtless significant that these instances were all in early texts.

On the matter of whether dying tradition were more formulaic in the way Holzapfel suggested Andersen felt unable to agree. Formulas are present, and probably in equal quantities, in both dying and innovative traditions: the important thing was what the individual singers did with them, and in this sense it was difficult to accept that a good singer was less 'traditional' than a bad one; the formulas themselves have an innovative potential, which may or may not be exploited.

To a question on whether 'dying' and 'growing' traditions were not rather romantic concepts, and what precisely he meant by the former, Holzapfel replied that a tradition must be considered as dying when the singers no longer sang the songs in the natural course of their social lives, but only when prompted by a collector, as in the case of Evald Tang Kristensen's informants. There followed a brief exchange on whether this was indeed the case with the singers referred to.

Iørn Piø intervened to note that Flemming G. Andersen's results were independent of this problem, as he concentrated on narrative technique, and went on the ask Holzapfel if, in view of his own work on the 'epic formula' he was happy with Andersen's notion of 'supra narrative' functions. Holzapfel agreed that it was 'useful'. Flemming G. Andersen observed that the materials they investigated in search of formulas differed: his were restricted to ballads, while Holzapfel in addition explored other forms of literature and pictorial sources - but this, Holzapfel interjected, was precisely to find the forerunners of the ballad formulas. Andersen went on to stress the value of asking the singers themselves for their views: in his experience they acknowledged that the formulas have a distinct and appreciated role in story-telling.

Viggo Hjørnager Pedersen invited the speakers to offer their definition of the ballad. Flemming G. Andersen responded that for him it was a dramatic narrative in song which told its story through a combination of formulas and context-bound phrases, arranged according to conceptual and verbal patternings. This should not however be taken as the definition of the genre but as a description of a narrative mode: it is instructive to see that in the cases of songs known to have been composed initially as broadside ballads, with few such balladic characteristics, these become more prominent in versions recorded later from oral tradition.

In response to David Buchan's query if the concept of 'thrift', mooted by the oral-formulaic theorists, was useful in the ballad formula context Flemming G. Andersen agreed that to a degree it was, at least with regard to tradition as a whole: the existence of formulas implied a limitation in the range of variation of expression, leaving some of the elaboration to be performed on the supra-narrative level. But it was less useful as applied to individual singers, who were less 'thrifty', and varied their formulas more, than might have been expected. Andreas Haarder asked if such thrift in ballad tradition - the cutting-out of unneccessary matter which instead was supplied at the supra-narrative level - together with the use of formulas for this purpose, might not have been influenced by not-balladic traditions, for example folk tales. Andersen was doubtful if this could be the case: the sheer consistency of the formulaic system within balladry suggested rather than it was intrinsic to the tradition itself.

Reimund Kvideland suggested that these supra-narrative levels and functions might be seen in terms of a 'meta-language'. Flemming G. Andersen thought this might be going too far - the supra-narrative qualities of the formulas were very closely linked to their narrative content.

Following Iørn Piø's invitation to elaborate on the value of speaking to the singers themselves, Andersen noted that they could provide significant insights, provided they were not led by the interviewer. Sven-Bertil Jansson agreed and added that they could likewise be appealed to in resolving the question discussed in the preceding session, the concept of the type: how do the singers distinguish one song from another? Vésteinn Ólason warned that the singers should not be relied upon entirely for guidance, for example in this matter of types, or even on the question of generic distinctions. It was necessary to operate with two distinct systems: the 'ethnic genres' acknowledged by the singers, and the 'analytic genres' recognized by scholars. Piø noted that Svend Grundtvig in compiling *Danmarks gamle Folkeviser* did not apply the concept of type in the modern sense; his was an entirely practical arrangement of the texts.

David Buchan, prompted by the reference to 'ethnic' and 'analytic' genres, asked if Flemming G. Andersen was concerned at having taken an analytic genre, the Child ballad canon, as the basis for his investigations, rather than an ethnic genre, say the 'muckle sangs' of the Scottish travellers, although in this instance the two seemed to correspond. Andersen accepted the point, and noted that indeed his main traveller informant, Lizzie Higgins, included non-balladic songs in her concept of 'muckle sangs'. Buchan suggested that this may have been a personal idiosyncracy: for her mother, Jeannie Robertson, and the rest of the family, the 'muckle sangs' corresponded to the kind of ballads found in the Child collection. The matter certainly underlined the importance of getting to know the singers, their ideas and their backgrounds.

Otto Holzapfel observed that the problems of genre and type were interrelated, instancing the case of the German "Graf und Nonne": about 1,500 of the c. 2,000 recorded versions were in the 'classic' ballad mode, but the remainder were not - they were merely love songs. They nonetheless clearly belonged to the same ballad-type: 'type', then, was not even restricted to a single song-genre.

Session 4

Tradition and Text

Written paper
BY VÉSTEINN ÓLASON

"The concept of tradition in ballad research" is a well chosen topic for a symposium: it is a basic concept to which we must constantly return for revision and clarification; moreover, it has long been controversial and is likely to evoke mutual feelings of aggression between the camps of the folklorists and the literary scholars.

I should point out that I am not trained as a folklorist, but rather in the field of literary studies. I have, however, for many years been working with ballads, texts which are considered folklore no less than literature. When it comes to the study of older texts, there is obviously a border area where both disciplines can and should be applied, and where, in fact, it is not always easy to distinguish between the two. Nowhere has the cooperation of literary and folkloristic methods of study been more fruitful (at least in terms of the quantity of work published) than in ballad studies. This cooperation has been fruitful exactly because of a certain disharmony, or conflict of interests, between the two disciplines. Both disciplines have changed in the course of time, often under the influence of the same general trends in humanistic studies, but also because they have been pulled in different directions by other disciplines dealing with related fields, as for example in recent years, when literary studies have been heavily influenced by linguistics while the influence of social anthropology has been strong among folklorists. (This is of course not absolute, since folklorists have also been influenced by structuralist linguistics, as have some literary historians been by social anthropology, but I think as a description of general trends, it is acceptable.)

Underlying the differences between scholars from these two fields is, I think, a different attitude toward tradition, or rather, to the relationship between text and tradition. I should therefore like to look more closely at this relationship, because precisely there lies the importance of the concept of tradition in ballad scholarship for the student of literature.

Tradition is clearly not a strictly definable term, and the range of its reference is wide. However, I think everyone would agree that by it is meant that something is handed over from one generation to another, most often through many generations. In the wide sense of cultural and literary tradition, the term covers diverse phenomena, including written texts, but among folklorists there is a tendency to use the term only about what is not written, and in what follows I shall use it in that sense.

When dealing with a ballad tradition, a literary scholar is inclined to think only of the words, but this is a far too narrow concept of tradition. The words were a part of a wider context, one involving different kinds of activities: the poem was generally sung, with or without accompaniment, perhaps even in connection with certain movements, such as dance. The performance also belonged to a certain setting, a wedding, an evening of work at a farm, some sort of social occasion. Finally, each item of tradition forms part of a larger whole: the culture in which they were produced and received. Even this incomplete description shows what a difficult concept tradition is, an impression most certainly confirmed by the "Final discussion" printed in *Trends in Nordic Tradition Research*.

But the student of oral tradition, needs something more tangible to deal with, and the text has often seemed to form a concretization of tradition that was a suitable or tractable object for his study. There is no need to recapitulate here the story of how a philological text-concept came to dominate tradition research in the 19th, and well into the present century, but I would like to give some attention to the revolt against "textual positivism" in recent decades in order to take issue with some trends I see as dominating our discussions at present.

In Europe at least, folklorists revolted relatively late against positivism, probably due to the overwhelming influence and apparent success of the "historical-geographical" or "Finnish" school. But, the revolt was bound to come in folkloristics as in related fields. This revolt, which I do not claim to know in all its aspects, was heavily influenced by methods developed in the social sciences, especially functionalism of various types, and, to some extent, by structuralism. The functionalist influence resulted in a change of emphasis from the text, with its codified tradition, to the human bearers of tradition (whom I hate to reduce to 'informants' even though it can be convenient), while influence from structuralism resulted in serious doubt about the concreteness and 'innocence' of the text.

The functionalist case, with regard to the study of folk song (including ballads), has been argued lucidly by Reimund Kvideland, and I should therefore like to take a critical look at his views. (I have, I must confess, no idea whether Reimund would agree with my characterization of his views as functionalistic, but I am using the concept in a broad sense.)

In an article in *Sumlen* 1982 and in the above-mentioned *Trends in Nordic Tradition Research* Reimund has summed up the changes that have been taking place in folklore studies during the last decades. He emphasizes, quite correctly, that the study of folk song for a long time was, and to a great extent still is, characterized by a philosophical essentialism based on the notion that the concept of "ballad" denotes an essential universal object, as opposed to the nominalist attitude, which assumes that the concept is a scholarly creation. He points out a tendency to give up this essentialism, a tendency which he thinks amounts to a shift of paradigm in Kuhn's sense. Quoting the musical ethnologist Artur Simon, he describes it as resulting in a change of focus

> from evolutionism to culturalism,
> from historical study to cultural anthropology,
> from formalism to the study of socio-cultural context,
> from text analysis to the analysis of process,
> from the comparison of variants to the analysis of
>   repertory,
> from focussing on a single genre to an expanded concept of
>   folk song,
> from esthetic analysis to functional analysis,
> from literary to folkloristic analysis. 1)

1.   Trends in Nordic Tradition Research, eds. Honko and Laakso-
      nen, Studia Fennica 27, Helsinki, 1983, p. 177.

He comes to the conclusion that "... we have to rid ourselves of our infatuation with the text" and, further on:

> Our point of departure should not be song considered as ideal type or category, but rather the concrete phenomenon that people sing. The object of study must be primarily the fact of singing, considered as cultural expression. That means that the primary material for study does not consist of songs qua text or musical objectification, but rather of the functional context in which the songs are found. 2)

This may sound very exciting, but I see it as a severe limitation, even an impoverishment of folk song studies, if we are to give our main attention to the fact *that* people sing but consider it somehow less important *what* they sing. The benefit of this change of focus escapes me. On the other hand I see great disadvantages implicit in it when we are dealing with older material (when the singers are dead, to put it bluntly).

It may be that I am twisting Reimund's words, and I certainly do not deny the importance of the study of functional context, when we have access to it. Text acquires meaning only in some kind of context. In this respect there is a great difference in the situation of the scholar who is studying modern folk song and the one who is occupied with old ballads found only in manuscripts, often without any indication of the tune and more often than not without any information about a functional context. If we accept Reimund's description of our task, it seems obvious that the ballad scholar should concentrate on areas where the genre is still alive, if such can be found, or at least with traditions where the functional context is fairly fully documented in accordance with the needs of a modern folklorist. One must then ask if a study of ballad texts from the 16th to the 18th or even 19th centuries is worth while at all.

In this connection it is interesting to see what social anthropology today has to say about the study of myths in their functional context. In a recent essay Sir Edmund Leach describes his attitude toward the study of myth in the following way:

2.   Op.cit., pp. 181-182.

> Social anthropologists of my sort lay great stress on the fact that most of the evidence they use has been obtained at first hand by direct visual observation and by the direct recording of verbal utterances. We do not ignore literary evidence altogether, but we are very skeptical about the possibility of making ethnographic sense of literary texts which have been divorced from their original context of time and space. 3)

He continues:

> All this can be summarized by saying that, from the viewpoint of a social anthropologist such as myself, myth loses all meaning if it is taken out of context. It also loses a great deal of its meaning as soon as it is transformed from a sequence of verbal utterances into a literary text. 4)

Leach is here talking about myths, while we are discussing ballads, but it appears to me that a ballad or a folktale could easily function as myth in the sense used by him. If we accept his conclusions, which I find quite convincing, it follows that a ballad scholar who takes the social anthropological model seriously, has only one possibility open to him, i.e., to study a community where ballads are sung as part of a living tradition. This seems to be the only way that can enable a scholar to form theories or make scientifically valid generalizations about the ballad as a social and anthropological phenomenon. Attempts at making such generalizations on the basis of literary record only would be doomed to failure from the start.

But what are we then to do with our heritage, *Danmarks gamle Folkeviser*, *Child*, etc.? Are we to throw them out of the window, burn the archives, as an eminent Danish folklorist is reported to have suggested? Although this radical solution to the ballad problem might please officials who are desperately seeking to make cuts in the budgets of academic institutions, I do not subscribe to it. Our answer must be to accept the object of our study for what

3. M.I. Steblin-Kamenskij, Myth. Critical Introduction by Sir Edmund Leach. Ann Arbor, 1982, p. 4.
4. Op.cit., p. 6.

it is, namely texts. In many cases, e.g. in the case of the Icelandic ballads, the corpus of texts is almost all that remains of a once existing and functioning ballad tradition. I don't have to say that this is something I regret, and that I consider the study of living ballad traditions to be extremely important and illuminating also for the study of dead ones, but if we want to go on studying ballad texts from former centuries we should accept them for what they are.

But, we return to the texts with a lot of problems unsolved. Even if we accept, however reluctantly, the texts as our objects of study, we still face the need for some context in which to place the texts. The most immediate context is tradition. It is inevitable, especially if we want to distinguish in some way between texts derived from oral tradition and the texts of literary tradition, to try to find out as much as we can about the oral background for the ballad texts. The texts themselves are not oral tradition, but they are, when they are faithfully recorded, footprints or fossils of the living tradition, preserving semantic structures that once existed as manifestations of that tradition. The ballad scholar is in a difficult situation when he wants to interpret and analyse these structures. Basically, his problem is the same as that of any interpreter of texts, but his possibilities are more limited than those of a scholar dealing with a purely literary text, if his aim is the recovery of an 'original' meaning. He has more unknown factors to deal with. But the difficulty of this position should not be overemphasized. It appears formidable if we concentrate on a single text and want to establish a dialogue with the 'sender' of its message. But the ballad scholar ought to realize more easily than the literary scholar dealing with a text written by a known author that the text speaks with more than one voice; in it other texts are echoed, and in them still other texts. This play of echoes and the systems or codes that make it possible is in fact the phenomenon that appears to us as tradition: our quarry.

I have no doubt that you have heard in these last words an echo of Roland Barthes, but as his theories are well known I see no reason to elaborate.

In opposition to the movement away from the text called upon by the functionalist, I think that a renewed interest in the text and in the comparison of texts is of vital importance for the student of ballad tradition. It may well be that the comparison of variants of individual ballad types and their geographical distribution is a line of study which will not lead any further than it has done already. I think, however, that applied with an awareness of its limitations, this method can in many cases help us to verify or overthrow generally accepted theories of the history of the ballad genre, and I think that we need to know as much about the chronology and geography of this history as it is possible to find out. But a revised concept of the text, together with the post-structuralist concept of intertextuality offer possibilities for new lines of study which may be the shortest route to some understanding of ballad tradition and its social context. This is a field where the concept of intertextuality is of obvious importance because of the conventionality of ballad language, I mean language in the widest sense, including the application of formulae and conventional narrative structures and themes. In the same way, an analysis of the deeper semantic structures of ballad texts, which only appear through work with a large number of texts, as opposed to the structural analysis of individual ballads, which it is extremely difficult to control, could yield important knowledge of the tradition.

However, you may ask, is there not a contradiction between a text-model borrowed from post-structuralism and an attempt to see the ballad as an historical phenomenon? My answer is no, not if we avoid going to the extreme of isolating language and meaning from the material world in which we live, act and speak (or sing). Studies in the ballad traditions of pre-industrial societies are of course only a small part of a larger project of humanistic studies in which there is room for many approaches. It would seem an anachronism to me if students of the ballad tradition should look away from the texts at a time when the concept of the text has become more dynamic than it has ever been before, when new methods in the study of texts open up the possibility of discerning in the interplay of texts an underlying historical dialectic.

Finally, I should like to clarify my position on some important points:

1) Although I see it as important to gather knowledge about the bearers of tradition, the singers in our case, and their personal and social circumstances, I find that the results of such studies are often difficult to connect in any meaningful way with the actual texts and that they cannot replace studies of the texts themselves.

2) Studies of the repertoires of individual singers are also important and may often help to detect intertextual relationships between different genres. But repertoire studies must go hand in hand with text studies, and when we have little or no information about the repertoire of individual ballad singers, we should not let that reduce our interest in the texts gathered from them.

3) Although I readily admit that no clearcut lines can be drawn between ballads and other types of folk song, and ballad studies may well be pursued in combination with a more comprehensive approach, I think that the 'balladic' nature of certain texts has been, or can be, established with sufficient certainty to justify the concept of ballad as an object for study.

4) Purely literary or aesthetic analysis of ballad texts has limited scientific value, especially when applied to isolated texts or types without regard to ballad conventions and other contextual information. However, it may help to define the 'meaning' of a text and hence its possible functions.

5) The most direct way to the knowledge of the ballad tradition lies through the texts themselves, which are real and present while the tradition in many cases is beyond reach. Contextual studies can be of immense help but there is no way around the actual texts.

Háskóli Íslands, Reykjavík

Oral presentation by *Vésteinn Ólason*

In my paper I have reacted against a tendency to see context as more important than text. The reasons for this tendency are in themselves easy to understand: in the past many scholars have neglected to take the context into account in their ballad studies; moreover, it may have caused some irritation among folklorists that the study of old ballads has dominated folk song studies in Scandinavia to such a large extent. Be that as it may, it is a fact that many people are interested in what we call folk ballads or traditional ballads, and in the study of these, I maintain, there is no way around the recorded texts, and no reason to avoid them since there is still a lot of questions which ballad scholarship ought to answer and cannot answer without more work with the texts themselves. When the singers and their culture are gone, the most direct way of reaching them is through the texts.

Without going into detail I suggest that a post-structuralist concept of text opens up possibilities and perspectives of vital importance to ballad scholars which they have only just begun to explore.

I do not think that there is any fundamental difference or contradiction between the project I should like to see realized in ballad studies and the project called upon by the 'functionalists' or 'contextualists'. Underlying both is an idea of a dialectical relationship between system and process that is ultimately derived from linguistics. Therefore these lines of research should go hand in hand and support each other. This view was in fact corroborated by the three papers presented yesterday and the following discussions.

Although I did not consider it necessary to elaborate upon the text concept I apply in my paper, it may be helpful for the discussion if I briefly do so now:

1. The text should not be seen as some kind of solid object an isolated "structure of meaning", but rather as a structure of signs symbolizing and act of communication involving several factors which we can (with Jakobson) specify as addresser - context - message - code - canal - addressee. The text not only delivers the message but it incorporates the relations between these factors and should be studied with reference to all of them.

2. The consequence of this approach is that in interpreting the

'meaning' of a text one has to proceed in a dialectial way, working out the relations between individual factors as well as their relations to the whole process. Although this model may seem abstract it opens up the possibility of analysing the text in its historical context, since its meaning is produced (by the addresser) and reproduced (by the addressee) in a specific place at a specific time. In these historical events system and process are united. The recording of a folklore text presents an especially complicated case. On the one hand, the singer is (more or less freely) reproducing something he/she has received; on the other hand, we have to distinguish between the original addressee (the audience), the recorder, and the interpreter (the scholar).

3. Interpretation is not the only aim of the student of the text. He wants to discover the conditions of the text, the conditions of signification through a particular medium, say a ballad. Here, a crucial point is the dependence of any text upon other texts. The context of Jakobson's model, referred to above, often understood as the 'world' the text refers to, must be seen as largely pre-formed into texts. The conditions of the primary text, the object of study, must then be sought in the codes governing the production of meaning by addresser and addressee. In the case of a ballad text, the primary context for establishing the codes is a corpus of ballad texts forming a ballad discourse, while the specificity of this discourse can only be defined in relation to other kinds of discourse functioning in the culture the ballads are derived from. We can put this more simply by saying that in the study of ballads recorded in the sixteenth or seventeenth centuries, but supposed to have medieval roots, it is important to study not only ballads but also other types of texts, such as romance, religious song, etc., etc. It is, of course, not necessary to use the same terminology as I have here borrowed from the structuralists. We can say that we want to study ballad conventions, the distinctly balladic or balladesque, and ballad scholars should be among the first to accept the idea that a text grows out of other texts, the idea of intertextuality.

**Opposition by *Lise Præstgaard Andersen*
(Notes by Thomas Pettitt)**

Lise Præstgaard Andersen expressed her general agreement with Ólason's paper, and felt likewise that it was compatible with the approaches urged by Kvideland. Ólason, as a literary historian, saw ballads as texts like other literature, whereas Kvideland preferred the 'singing activity' approach. The latter is of course more difficult in dealing with the earlier materials, but Ólason acknowledges the importance of both text and context, of combining literary analysis with exploration of contextual factors (singers, repertoires, etc.), of seeing the text as a 'footprint', the record of a past event. The question then is how to combine literary and folkloristic, aesthetic and historical approaches to the same text.

Danish ballad research has considered the substance of the ballads as both documents in the history of ideas and as reflections of human concerns which have remained constant through the centuries. Their form has been generally considered to be characterized by formulaic language and repetitions: a highly conventional vehicle for expression which at first sight does not promise much by way of the originality normally expected of great literature. The people of the Middle Ages, it seems, enjoyed repetition – familiar topics expressed in familiar phrases. Modern tastes are different, but this does not mean that the medieval ballads are museum-pieces. They can still be enjoyed and appreciated, for repetition can be used skilfully, both to satisfy by fulfilling expectations and to startle by not doing so. Lise Præstgaard offered some instances of Danish ballads where telling modifications of formulaic expressions were appreciated as art: we need not always demand originality. And even the most conventional qualities of the ballads were still appreciated, in different spheres, today: as Vésteinn Ólason suggested in an earlier session, the ballads' topics of sensational events, violence and blood are still devoured avidly by readers of the popular press, and it may be added that their repetitive, formulaic quality has been sustained in popular 'B' movies. So ballads are more than 'footprints': they can be enjoyed as aesthetic experiences.

Discussion. Notes by *Thomas Pettitt*

Iørn Piø complimented Vésteinn Ólason on the commonsense and clarity of his presentation, but wondered if he and Lise Præstgaard Andersen were really in such agreement with each other as had just been professed. Ólason had conceded the limited value of purely literary studies; Lise Præstgaard had urged that ballads could indeed be appreciated as good literature. Ólason observed that in equating the ballads with the sensational press he had been thinking of the use to which they were put: this did not imply equating the two in aesthetic terms. Lise Præstgaard agreed that both forms fulfilled a human craving for the sensational.

Minna Skafte Jensen offered some remarks on the discussion from the point of view of Homeric studies. Here too there seemed to be a general tendency to search for the oldest layers of tradition, and because they were the oldest, not because they were better. Ólason interjected that he meant old ballads, not old versions. Minna Skafte Jensen went on to observe the dangers of generalization about the ballads which survive in similar texts but which nonetheless handle materials in quite different ways, as in the case of the "Cherry Tree Carol" instanced in an earlier session by Thomas Pettitt, with different texts offering significantly different taleroles for a main character. Given the general conventions, the impact of thwarting these conventions is so much the greater. It is interesting that Homeric studies, which lack texts, and ballad scholarship, which has so many, should encounter the same problem of correlating the individual text to tradition: perhaps it would help to appeal to the linguistic concepts of *langue* and *parole*. Vésteinn Ólason emphasized the necessity of a dialectical approach which explored the relationship between the text as an entity and the tradition behind it.

David Buchan intervened to suggest that some confusions might be resolved by abandoning the term 'text', which had too many literary overtones, and speaking instead of a 'version' which was not an entity in itself but part of a larger entity, the 'type', itself a part of tradition. Minna Skafe Jensen emphatically disagreed: in the case of the "Cherry Tree Carol" it was clear that there were two distinct texts, each with its own inner integrity, not such versions of some superior 'type'. 'Version' and 'text' were both necessary concepts, depending on the precise phenomena being investigated. There is no sense in calling the *Iliad* a 'version', even though it is traditional. Ólason, prompted by the suggestion of another participant that much of the terminology be done away with, substituting 'words', say, for 'version' and 'texts', defended the existing terminology despite its confusions and difficult connotations.

Sven-Bertil Jansson observed that he preferred the term 'song' – a useful reminder of the musical aspect of the ballads which the conference had sadly neglected. The ballads are sung; they have to fit a melody. The song is part of a tradition, but is still a song; the singer thinks of it in this way, and is not concerned how many versions there are. So if we have problems of interpretation we should ask the singers.

Tore Nyberg agreed that 'text' had too many connotations to be useful, and this applied to historical research as well. Each 'version' has its own value, and will depend on the moment and the singer. Otto Holzapfel remarked that it would be easy enough to change the terms, less so the thinking behind them: things would carry on in much the same way. Much of the confusion results from the different research traditions: early German scholarship, the kind which produced the *Household Tales* and *Wunderhorn* was essentially a business of editing texts; Danish scholarship too, thanks to the availability of the early manuscripts, has been somewhat text-oriented, and has rather neglected oral traditions. It is probably best to restrict the term 'variant' to material collected from tradition: a song consists of variants, and every variant is a text.

Kirsten Sass Bak agreed with Jansson that musical aspects of ballad tradition had been unduly neglected. 'Singing activity' was a useful concept, as it insists on the musical aspect, which has its own problems. Iørn Piø insisted that one could call a text whatever one wished, it remained a text. 'Variant' was unfortunate, in that it implied a standard which had somehow been varied from. The example of French singing-games was referred to, in which the music remains constant, while the words change according to the immediate circumstances. Responding to Piø, Otto Holzapfel noted that 'variant' implied variation not from a standard, but from an ideal: the text is a result of innovation and continuity, so it is a variant. We must apply the available terminology. Ólason agreed: 'type' is fairly well defined in scholarly tradition; a variant is a single recording; groups of similar variants are versions. It was suggested that we must first decide to what purpose we study the ballads - pleasure, eternal values, the singer, their society: this should determine the terminology applied.

There followed a confused discussion of the purposes of ballad study, the most memorable contribution being Vésteinn Ólason's observation, 'big questions provoke small answers'.

Session 5

Oral Tradition
– Literary Tradition

Written paper
BY IØRN PIØ

Already in his first studies on ballads from 1846, *Engelske og skotske Folkeviser*, Svend Grundtvig was engrossed in that which is an essential characteristic feature of the concept of tradition: the interplay between variation and stability. He put it in other words, but this is what he means, just as it is clear that for him tradition means oral tradition.

In the following year, when he published his *Plan til en ny udgave af Danmarks gamle Folkeviser*, he emphasised that he would re-print *only* those ballads which "had been transmitted orally to the present day". He is quite aware that "much which this source has yielded originates in the old printed collections and in the broadsheets", but that it "is not difficult to judge" which ballads are involved.

When he published "Agnete og havmanden" 10 years later he printed at the same time a broadsheet from the eighteenth century as principal text (DgF 38 Aa) and notes as variants 9 references which "on the whole" correlate "closely with the text of the broadsheet" (DgF 38 Ab-k). It may appear inconsistent, but is not so. Grundtvig considers DgF "a variant of the previous (DgF 37 "Jomfruen og dværgekongen") or rather a transitional form between this and the subsequent ballad" (DgF 39 "Nøkkens svig").

The fact that some of the singers who in the 19th century sang "Agnete og havmanden" mixed it together with "Jomfruen og dværgekongen", plus the fact that "Agnete og havmanden" has a number of features in common with "Nøkkens svig" is for Grundtvig sufficient grounds to consider this triple-ballad complex one tradition which throughout the centuries from the middle ages up until the present day has assumed different forms.

The reason for Grundtvig's being able to believe this can only be that, inspired by E.G. Geijer and F. . Herder, he thought that ballads such as the three just mentioned, together with the 536 others which were published in his *Danmarks gamle folkeviser*, emerged in some way or other in the Middle Ages "as living organisms".

At times Grundtvig says of a ballad from *DgF* that young it may be, but it comes from an old family. This is what he feels about "Agnete og havmanden", and the closest members of the family can be said to be "Jomfruen og dværgekongen" and "Nøkkens svig". They are variations "or rather" different forms of the same tradition, and this tradition has an individual author, "but he is only the instigator of" the ballad's "first appearance", "later (the ballad) was elaborated and in many ways transformed in its progress from mouth to mouth, from land to land"; through the oral tradition "it has come eventually to us, with its testimony, which from generation to generation developed it and transmitted it."

Read with sympathy this is expressed excellently and precisely. We understand clearly that as a researcher he was not interested in tradition which stemmed from printed sources, but he published it just as seriously as those ballads which had only been "orally transmitted".

In recent years, however, there has been an increasing tendency to consider the relationship between the oral and printed tradition. Put in another way: the question as to what extent the interplay between variability and stability is dependent on printed sources - not least on broadsheet ballads.

This problem has been long known in Germany. Hermann Strobach wrote an excellent exposé on this subject i 1981, *Zum geschichtlichen Stellenwert mündlicher und schriftlicher Überlieferung in der Volksliedtradition*. Referring to Rolf W. Brednich, he writes that: "Es ist ja bekannt, dass seit der Erfindung des Buchdruckes Liederbücher gedruckt worden sind, die dem praktischen Gebrauch dienten und einen bedeutenden Einfluss auf das umlaufende Liedgut hatten."

In Germany the earliest preserved printed ballads are from the 15th century, in Scandinavia they are from the first decades of the 16th century. It is quite obvious that many of these shoddy publications were thrown away immediately after use, that is to say after the ballads had been learnt by heart. And it is significant that the oldest preserved publications involve ballads in connection with the battle between Catholics and Lutherans in the 1520s and 1530s: this was a subject which rose considerably above the level of light verse, which must also have been produced, and accounts for it having been preserved by historically interested collectors.

The question is, however, whether ballad researchers can tell historians interested in book production something about the broadsheet industry, the actual production of which is not directly preserved but which is transcribed in the oldest ballad manuscripts, and which has influenced the oral tradition as early as the 16th century. In my opinion it is possible to do so.

I personally feel that as far as research into ballads is concerned it is meaningless to use the date of the reformation, 1536, as the closing date of the Middle Ages in Denmark. More important in our connection is the invention of the art of printing in the 15th century and the spread of printing in the 16th century.

During my studies of the ballads which were published in *DgF* I distinguish between the ancient ballads from before c. 1500 and more recent popular ballads, i.e., broadsheets with ballads in the old ballad style which originally came onto the market *after* c. 1500. The year 1500 has been chosen because it is first thereabouts that we can in all probability allow ourselves to reckon on a production of ballads in Denmark.

This distinction, which I have attempted to substantiate in my book *Nye Veje til Folkevisen* (New Approaches to the Ballad), will influence an understanding of the concept of tradition within the field of ballad research. To put it simply, it can be said that the ancient ballads are traditional ballads, whereas the more recent popular ballads are what John Meier in 1906 called "Kunstlieder im Volksmunde".

For the sake of completeness I should add that I demonstrate that a number of ballads in *DgF* are neither old nor more recent popular ballads, but are, on the contrary, aristocratic ballads which were inspired by the old and more recent ballad tradition and which never really left the environment of the upper classes where they were composed and sung; and if they have left this environment it is because first and foremost Peder Syv published them in 1695; and after this edition the producers of broadsheet ballads reprinted them and when people sang these ballads they became "Kunstlieder im Volksmunde".

However, this symposium is chiefly concerned with the relationship between old and more recent ballads.

First, a few words on how I feel it is possible to tell whether
the ballad originally appeared orally or in a published form; if the
variation between the versions known from the popular tradition in
the 16th century is small, their common source *could* be found in a
broadsheet; if on the other hand the variation between the versions
known from the popular tradition in the 16th century is so great
that it is meaningless to presuppose a common source, then we
have old popular ballads, medieval ballads. To put it another way:
if one can observe - indeed if one can reconstruct - the original
form of the ballad, then it is originally a broadsheet ballad; if one
cannot, then it is an old popular ballad, or rather old popular ballad
tradition or, even better, old sung-recited ballad-tales.

As far as the more recent popular ballads are concerned, Axel
Olrik has already retorted by writing that what I succeed in finding
is "the oldest form we can reach by inference" equals "the common
original form for the existing variants" and equals "the basic form
in practice", and he assumes fundamentally that behind this there
is an old popular ballad tradition. I do not. I feel I can establish
that since the 16th century and right up to the close of the 18th
century, ballads have been written anew in the old popular ballad
style.

By isolating a large number of ballads from *DgF* as originally
broadsheet ballads, I have, moreover, immediately placed a great
part of the Danish ballad tradition within a European context.
There is now no longer anything special with the Danish traditions
seen in relationship to those of, for example Germany, England or
Scotland. It was believed that there was something special as long
as it was impressed on us that our medieval ballads were originally
high literary aristocratic ballads which had come down in the world
to a popular level. This view results among other things from our
not having been able to understand what ballad traditions are
actually found in our famous manuscripts of the nobility from c.
1550 until c. 1650.

Old popular ballad tradition is also found in these manuscripts,
but as a rule it has been adapted in a literary manner, whereas I
have been able to isolate a number of writers in Vedel's ballad
collection, writers who have collected unadapted popular ballads in
the 16th century. It is to a great extent through this discovery that

I have been able to isolate not only old, but also more recent material 300 years prior to that of the popular ballad collections of the 19th century.

Although my main purpose in *Nye Veje* is to study the ballads as folk songs from the 16th century up to the present day, I have also - as an extension of the theory relating to the broadsheet ballad - in a final chapter advanced a theory concerning the origin of the old tradition of ballads. I believe that the medieval ballad originates in the markets, where the genre - or rather: the ballad narrative technique, as Holzapfel calls it - was created by the market singers.

This technique aims at an oral presentation of ballad tales, and thereby also at being appropriated orally by the audience. This applies above all to ballad tales which are sung-narrated in the 4-line verse, which I therefore call the *market verse*: here we find tales of Germanic mythological giants and their feats, and of the heroes and villains of Danish history.

The market verse employes a refrain which the audience can sing along with, but which the audience is not encouraged to dance to. On the other hand the audience is frequently encouraged to dance to the 2-line verse refrain, and what gives these dance ballads an interesting perspective is that they tell stories of the meeting of anonymous people with the supernatural or other dramatic events in their everyday life as well as jesting tales. I call the 2-line verse the *folk song verse*, and as the tales that are sung-narrated in this verse style are to a very considerable extent influenced by the social environment that they were sung in, this could be a further indication of this simpler verse form being that which folk singers have created, or at least have preferred: for a talented singer it was easy to manage. To sing-narrate a 2-line verse was almost like narrating a legendary tale or an anecdote. Here the singer could really get into his stride, as the folk song verse is an invitation to improvisation.

This is the perspective: the *improvised ballad tradition* with no or very little influence from the printed verse is found in the old 2-line folk ballad tradition, and *memorised ballads* are found in the more recent folk ballad tradition, in that the more recent folk ballads are originally "Kunstlieder im Volksmunde" - and thus it is only in the more recent tradition that it is reasonable to talk of, for example, "zersingen" or what newer folklore ballad research calls "umsingen".

And in the old folk ballad in the 4-line verse, which was originally introduced orally as "tribune art", we find the *memorised tradition with the possibility for improvisation without the influence of printed sources*, in so far as no producers of broadsheet ballads appear to have printed these old market ballads.

To give some examples:

in the old popular ballads "Elverskud", "Jomfruen og dværgekongen" and "Hr. Bøsmer i elverhjem" we find the improvised ballad tradition;

in the more recent ballads "Niels Ebbesøn", "Ebbe Skammelsøn", "Stolt Ellensborg" and "Hr. Tønne af Alsø", we find the memorised ballads;

in the old market ballads "Mordet i Finderup lade", "Marsk Stig og de fredløse", "Holger Danske og Burmand" and "Angelfyr og Helmer Kamp" we find the memorised tradition without the influence of printed sources.

Danish Folklore Archives and Odense University

Discussion. Notes by *Elisabeth Vestergaard*

Bengt R. Jonsson questioned Piø's theory that ballads were printed on broadsheets as early as in 1520. Printing was a new means of mass-production and transmission, not as highly esteemed as manuscripts, and he suggested that broadsheets were more concerned with the reformation debate and religious propaganda than with ballads.

In response Piø pointed out that only broadsheets dealing with important religious events would have been preserved by book collectors, and that the more common ones would have been thrown away. He raised the question of literacy in the sixteenth century and stated that even a low figure of literacy would be sufficient for a broadsheet production since ballads would have been known by the people anyway.

Jonsson wanted to have it confirmed that 'production of ballads' meant 'printing', and referring to p. 105 of Piø's paper he urged Piø to elaborate on his division of the Danish ballad corpus into ballads composed before 1500 and those composed later. This division, he claimed, would remove a large number of Danish ballads from the main stream of balladry, and would do away with most of the Danish aristocratic ballad manuscripts. Piø replied that in some cases it was possible to recover the original form of a ballad, and unlike Axel Olrik he would hesitate to believe that behind the oldest surviving form of a ballad there must be some even older. A ballad is not older than its oldest record, unless proved otherwise; and if it was possible to compose ballads in the sixteenth century, as is for instance the case with "Ebbe Skammelsøn", such ballads should not be regarded as medieval at all. He went on to say that ladies of the nobility would often manufacture ballads in the old style, and claimed that if a ballad looks very old it is new. These ladies would also copy ballads from broadsheets.

Jonsson would still hold the view that there may be older forms behind the oldest record of a ballad, and asked how Piø could know that ballads had been composed for market performances. Piø argued that there were differences in 'feeling' and narrative detail between the older and the younger type. And of all the 539 ballads in *Danmarks gamle Folkeviser* only a small portion can be demonstrated to be of considerable age, i.e., composed before 1500.

In a final reference to Piø's paper (p. 107) Jonsson pointed out that also what Piø terms the 'folk song verse' has an end refrain.

Michel Olsen intervened to note that in Italy broadsheets were printed as early as in 1476, and for England Thomas Pettitt made the observation that by the late fifteenth century there were a large number of broadsheets in circulation. He regretted that the Danish past seems to be so dark, and pointed to England, where there is more solid evidence as broadsheets had to be registered with the Company of Stationers from 1557 to 1709. Piø and Jonsson noted that the situation was different in Scandinavia, and Buchan mentioned that in Scotland it was not until the eighteenth century that there was a sufficient market for a large scale production of broadsheets. Religious pamphlets, on the other hand, had been available earlier.

Returning to Piø's discussion of Vedel's writers (p. 106) Viggo Hjørnager Pedersen asked about the criteria for the eventual selection of writers, and Piø replied that Vedel had himself noted that some of his ballads had been collected among the common people, but also the internal stylistic features made it clear that Vedel's manuscripts are not aristocratic manuscripts.

Session 6

Scherz und Spott in der dänischen Gesangtradition

Aufsatz
VON RITA PEDERSEN

Die volkstümliche Tradition ist im weitesten Sinne dieses Worts am stärksten gewesen in der Erzählung über die Begegnung zwischen dem Menschen und den übernatürlichen, naturmytischen Kräften. Für den Menschen kann das Dasein unüberwindlich und unmöglich zu bewältigen werden (dänisch: blive ikke til at komme om ved). Das Lied über "Hr. Oluf" (DgF 47: "Elverskud"),1) der die Wahl zwischen Untergang durch Tod oder Verzauberung (dän. bjergtagning) hat, ist ein Bild dieser Unüberwindlichkeit (dän. uoverkommelighed).

Der Versuch, diese Unüberwindlichkeit auszuhalten oder zu beseitigen - dadurch dass man sie darstellte, darüber erzählte oder sang - hat dazu beigetragen, eine Tradition zu begründen, die sich zwischen den alten Prosaformen, Sagen, Märchen, Anekdoten, Gespensterberichten und der poetischen Form, mit der sich unser Symposium beschäftigt, den (Volks)liedern oder (Volks)balladen, bewegt.

Die Sage erzählt, dass "der Nix" (dän. "Nøkken") verschwindet, wenn er beim Namen genannt wird. In dem kleinen isländischen Lied "Elenar ljóð" (ÍFkv 2, dän. Parallele: DgF 39, "Nøkkens Svig") 2) trifft "Elen" auf dem Heimweg den arglistigen Nix, der versucht, sie zu locken, aber sie antwortet: "Ég því ekki nenni" (was soviel heisst wie: "Ich möchte nicht, will nich, habe keine Lust dazu") und

1. DgF: Svend Grundtvig, Axel Olrik u.a.: Danmarks gamle Folke-viser I-XII, Kopenhagen: Universitets-jubilæets Danske Samfund, 1853-1976.
2. ÍFkv: Jón Helgason: Íslenzk fornkvæði I-VIII, Editiones Arnamagnæanæ Series B, vol. 10-17, Kopenhagen: Munksgaard/Reitzel, 1962-81.

"so hvarf han frá henni". Auf Island trägt "der Nix" auch den
Namen "Nennir", und deshalb verschwindet er als Elen "nenni" sagt.
Wenn das Unding - die Unüberwindlichkeit - beim Namen genannt
wird, ist es möglich, ihn von sich zu weisen.

Dort wo der allgemeine Mensch sich in der rauhen Wirklichkeit
des Alltags in Situationen befindet oder gerät, die es ihm erschwe-
ren, das Dasein zu bewältigen, können sie erträglich werden durch
Anwendung der Waffe des Narren (dän. narrens, askepusterens,
amlodens våben): *Verlächerlichung, Provokation, Ironisierung* - sei
dies dadurch, dass die Dinge auf einer entwaffnenden, direkten und
groben Weise beim rechten Namen genannt werden - oder sei es
dadurch, dass es wie bei Elen im obenerwähnten "Elenar ljóð"
geschieht, wo sie das Unding - die Unüberwindlichkeit - auf einer
zwiedeutigen, geheimnisvollen, verdeckten Weise von sich weist.

Ein Teil der erhaltenen dänischen Gesangtradition besteht aus
Liedern mit einem solchen Inhalt von scherzender, spottender,
provozierender, ironisierender oder parodierender Art. - Eine klei-
nere Anzahl dieser Lieder wurde in DANMARKS GAMLE FOLKE-
VISER (DgF) herausgegeben, aber der Rest - der weitaus grösste
Teil - wurde erst herausgegeben, als zuerst der Volkskundler Evald
Tang Kristensen (ETKr) 3) und danach der Liederforscher Hakon
Grüner-Nielsen (HGrN) 4) sich im Jahre 1901 bzw. 1927-28 der
Aufgabe annahmen, zwar nicht alles, aber doch einen Teil des
restlichen Materials herauszugeben. Mit diesen beiden Ausgaben
erhielten wir eine neue Gattungsbezeichnung neben den in DgF
schon bestehenden 'kæmpeviser', 'naturmytiske (=trylle-)viser', 'le-
gendeviser', 'historiske viser', 'ridderviser', 'romanviser', 'lyriske
viser', da die Bezeichnung 'skæmteviser' (Scherzlieder) jetzt offizi-
ell in die dänische Liedtradition eingeführt wurde.

3. DSk: Evald Tang Kristensen: Et Hundrede Gamle danske
    Skjæmteviser efter Nutidssang samlede og for Størstedelen
    optegnede af Evald Tang Kristensen, Århus: Jacob Zeuner,
    1901.
4. DS: Hakon Grüner-Nielsen: Danske Skæmteviser (Folkeviser og
    Litterær Efterklang) efter Visehaandskrifter fra 16.-18.Aarh.
    og Flyveblade I-II, Kopenhagen: Universitets-jubilæets Danske
    Samfund, 1927-28.

ETKr, der sich überwiegend für zeitgenössische Bauernerzäh-
lungen und Bauernlieder interessierte, gab 1901 ET HUNDREDE
GAMLE DANSKE SKJÆMTEVISER EFTER NUTIDSSANG heraus. -
Dieses neue Hundertliederbuch war wie das alte HUNDERTLIE-
DERBUCH (dän. HUNDREDVISEBOGEN),5) das gut 400 Jahre früh-
er (im Jahre 1591) von Anders Sørensen Vedel herausgegeben
wurde, eine Ausgabe mit ausgewählten Liedern.
   ETKr beginnt sein Vorwort im Buch wie folgt:

"Efter lang betænkning har jeg endelig bestemt mig til at
lade disse viser komme frem for dagens lys. Og dog er dette
ikke helt rigtigt sagt. Jeg vil nemlig for visse visers
vedkommende blot kunne give antydning af, at de er til, at
de synges mand og mand imellem, og at de endog har været
ret yndede ved selskabelige sammenkomster, men jeg har
ikke kunnet trykke dem, da de ikke kan læses. Jeg har
forgjæves brudt hovedet med, hvordan jeg skulde bære mig
ad med at lade sådanne viser komme frem i deres helhed,
uden at de skulde give alt for megen forargelse. Der har da
ikke været andet at gjøre end at lægge det meste af dem til
side. Jeg har ligeledes forgjæves ledt efter sidestykker til
flere af disse viser i samlinger fra vore nabolande. Viserne
må sikkert være der, men man må have været i den samme
forlegenhed som jeg."

("Nach langem Bedenken habe ich mich schliesslich dafür
entschieden, diese Lieder ans Tageslicht zu bringen. Und
doch ist dies nicht ganz richtig gesagt. Denn was gewisse
Lieder betrifft, werde ich nur andeuten können, dass sie
existieren, dass sie unter gewöhnlichen Leuten gesungen
werden und dass sie bei geselligen Zusammenkünften sogar
sehr beliebt gewesen sind. Es war mir jedoch nicht möglich,
sie abzudrucken, da sie nicht gelesen werden können. Ich
habe mir vergebens den Kopf damit zerbrochen, wie ich es
anstellen sollte, solche Lieder als Ganzes zu veröffentli-
chen, ohne dass sie all zu grossen Anstoss erregen sollten.

5.   Hundredvisebogen: Anders Sørensen Vedel: It Hundrede vduaal-
     de Danske Viser Om allehaande Merckelige Krigs Bedrifft oc
     anden seldsom Euentyr ...., Ribe: Hans Brun, 1591.

Deshalb bestand keine andere Möglichkeit, als die meisten
von Ihnen beiseite zu legen. Ich habe ebenfalls vergeblich
nach Gegenstücken zu mehreren dieser Lieder in Sammlungen unserer Nachbarländer gesucht. Es gibt ganz sicher
diese Lieder, aber man muss in der gleichen Verlegenheit
gewesen sein wie ich.")

Hier wird uns ganz klar gesagt, dass es in der Tradition des 19.
Jahrhunderts Lieder gibt, über die wir nicht direkt Kenntnis
erlangen können. Zweifellos hatten auch die Mitteiler Bedenken,
die sehr groben, derben Lieder vor dem Aufzeichner, dem Schul-
lehrer und dem Freund ETKr zu singen. ETKr weiss jedoch, dass es
sie gibt:

> "Jeg må udtale mig for Danmarks vedkommende. Der har
> været ikke så få gamle grove skjæmteviser hertil lands."

> ("Ich muss mich für Dänemark äussern: Es gibt nicht wenige
> alte derbe Scherzlieder hierzulande")

>   (fortgesetztes Zitat)

Die handgeschriebenen Aufzeichnungen von ETKr, aufbewahrt und
registriert in DANSK FOLKEMINDESAMLING, zeigen somit auch,
dass es ein erheblich grösseres Material an Scherzliedern gibt, als
es der Ausgabe nach den Anschein hat.

Dass zugleich eine Auswahl zwischen den Varianten der Liedern
getroffen worden ist, und zwar ohne ausführliche Anmerkungen,
bedeutet, dass diese Ausgabe von scherzenden Liedern aus dem 19.
Jahrhundert sich nur schwer von der Liedforschung verwenden
lässt. Sie kann nur ein Bild des Scherzgesanges des 19. Jahrhunderts
vermitteln, aber das Bild verzeichnet jedoch gleichzeitig diese
Liedtradition.

Als sich HGrN etwa 25 Jahre später vornahm, die Scherzlieder
aus dem 16.-18. Jahrhundert, die in Handschriften, Bauernlieder-
büchern und in Flugschriften überliefert sind, herauszugeben, be-
nutzte er ein ähnliches Verfahren bei der Edition, wie es bei DgF
verwendet wurde. Das Ergebnis wurde eine fast vollständige Ausgabe des damals bekannten Liedmaterials mit Haupttext, Varianten
und umfassenden Kommentaren. HGrN veröffentlichte nicht wieder
die Tradition des 19. Jahrhunderts sondern verwies teils auf die

Ausgabe von ETKr, teils auf die in DANSK FOLKEMINDESAMLING registrierten Aufzeichnungen von ETKr.

Aber wenn wir uns jetzt dieses ältere Material anschauen, müssen wir uns zwangsläufig Gedanken darüber machen, inwieweit auch dieses Traditionsbild korrekt ist. Man kann sich sehr wohl vorstellen, dass hier von Aufzeichnern und Flugschriftliederproduzenten eine ähnliche Aussortierung von besonders derbem Material vorgenommen worden ist, wie sie von Mitteilern und Aufzeichnern des 19. Jahrhunderts gemacht wurde. Uns wurden verhältnismässig wenige alte Scherzlieder überliefert: HGrN hat insgesamt 98 Liedtypen aus dem 16.-18. Jahrhundert registriert. Es stellt sich ferner heraus, dass nur wenige und - darauf komme ich später zurück - ganz spezielle Liederhandschriften scherzende Lieder mitteilen. Die Flugschriftliederproduktion ist erheblich grösser, wir können jedoch nicht ausschliessen, dass die in Kleindruck herausgegebenen Lieder (Flugschriften) in den Fällen redigiert waren, in denen eine mündliche Tradition als Vorlage verwendet wurde - und dass die Lieder, die direkt für den Druck verfasst wurden, in einem für die Zeit annehmbaren und anständigem Ton gehalten wurden. Wir müssen wiederum damit rechnen, dass die derbsten Lieder aussortiert sein können - mit dem Ergebnis, dass gerade die Lieder verschwanden, die bei den Zeitgenossen Anstoss erregen können hätten, weil sie direkt und provozierend auf Fehler in der Gesellschaft verwiesen und diese beleuchteten.

Die Lieder in den Handschriften des 16. und 17. Jahrhundets 6) deuten nicht unmittelbar auf solche Vorbehalte der Aufzeichner. Wo ein Scherzlied in den Handschriften in der Tradition des 19. Jahrhunderts wiedergefunden wird, ist es die alte Form, die Form der Handschrift, die die deftigste ist. Bemerkenswert ist es zu erfahren, dass es sich bei den Handschriften nicht ausschliesslich um Männer handelte, die diese derben Lieder einschrieben. In JENS BILLES VISEBOG aus dem Jahre 1555 hat Jens Billes Kusine, Anne Skave, ein Lied darüber, "was mein Mann hat und was er nicht hat" (DS 46 "Alle Mand og min Mand"), eingefügt. Dieses Lied ist was Sprachgebrauch und Gegenstand betrifft, erheblich direkter, als was in den Aufzeichnungen von ETKr zu finden ist.

6. DGF XII, Seite 299-403.

Wenn das Scherzliedmaterial in verhältnismässig wenigen der
alten Handschriften zu finden ist, so können wir nicht ohne
weiteres davon ausgehen, dass der Grund ein moralischer ist. Etwa
die grosse Liedersammlung aus dem Jahre 1570 (Archivbezeichnung: KAREN BRAHES FOLIO) mit über 200 Liedern, die vermutlich von der adligen Frau Margrethe Lange in Engelsholm gesammelt wurden, enthält trotz ihres Umfangs keine Scherzlieder. Die
Sammlerin hat zwar eine gewisse Neigung, ihren Liedredaktionen
eine geringfügige Veränderung in Richtung auf Wohlanständigkeit
zu geben, aber die Handschrift offenbart vor allen Dingen ein Be-
wusstsein, wie die Lieder der Sammlung aussehen sollen, und zwar
was die Form betrifft: die Liedform ist die Gattung des Volkslieds,
zwei- oder vierzeilige Strophen mit Kehrreim, und was den Inhalt
betrifft: die Geschichte der Lieder erzählen über die Taten von
adligen und königlichen Personen, über Liebeskummer, über Glück
und Unglück. Die Sammlerin ist mit einem modernen Ausdruck
gattungsbewusst, wie auch eine Vielzahl der Liederbuchanleger in
den Generationen danach.

Lieder, die auf eine direkte und provozierende oder auf eine
zwiedeutige und oft perfide, verdeckte Weise über den Bauern und
sein Leben erzählen, über die Beziehung zur Geistlichkeit, über
Machtmisbrauch, über Laster und soziale Not, haben dagegen
Personen mit einem realistischen Interesse für Gegenwart und
Gesellschaft über das Leben um 'breden bord' und 'i højenloft'
hinaus interessiert. Aber ein solches Interesse erfordert sowohl Mut
als auch eine gesellschaftlich gute Position. Wie schon erwähnt
befindet sich das Scherzliedmaterial im LIEDERBUCH DES JENS
BILLE (am Hof von Christian III, JENS BILLES VISEBOG), einer
kleinen privaten Sammlung von 88 Liedern, eine Sammlung, die
zugleich ein historisches Interesse beim Hauptaufzeichner Jens
Bille zeigt. Ferner finden wir Scherzliedmaterial in zwei Lieder-
büchern etwa aus dem Jahre 1620-30: SOPHIA SANDBERGS
HÅNDSKRIFT und IDE GIØES VISEBOG, die sich beide zusammen
mit JENS BILLES VISEBOG und MARGRETHE LANGES VISESAM-
LING Anfang des 17. Jahrhunderts auf dem Herrensitz Rosenholm
von Holger Rosenkrantz 'den Lærde' bei Aarhus befinden - ein
gelehrtes, literarisches Milieu von Welt, ein kleines 'Universitäts-
milieu', wo die hier genannten privaten Sammlungen verwendet und
gut aufbewahrt wurden.

IDE GIØES VISEBOG 7) mit 75 Liedern erhielt den Namen nach
der Nichte und Pflegetochter von Holger Rosenkrantz, Ide Giøe,
Schwester der Mette Giøe, Herausgeberin des Liederbuchs TRAGI-
CA aus dem Jahre 1657. Ide Giøe hat kaum selbst die Handschrift
erstellt, mehrere Schreiberhände haben hier gearbeitet. Die Handschrift kann von Sophie Brahe, der jüngeren Schwägerin der Margrethe Lange erstellt sein. Aber bei dem scherzenden Lied von
"Germand Smed og Præstens Datter" (DgF 368) mit dem wohlbe-
kannten Schweinehirten-Motiv hat Ide Giøe 'der Umwelt' mitge-
teilt, dass dies 'ihr eigenes Lied (Zitat: "min Uise egen") ist. Das
Lied, das sich in der Tradition des 19. Jahrhunderts wiederfindet,
ist nur eines von vielen guten Beispielen dafür, was diese Handschrift an alter, jütländischer, volkstümlicher und vermutlich
mündlich überlieferter Tradition repräsentiert. Auf Rosenholm gab
es ein Interesse für Volkskunde, das uns heute zugute kommt.
Vielleicht war der Abstand zwischen dem Adel des Herrensitzes
und den schlichteren Verhältnissen nicht grösser, als dass Lieder,
die bei den Bauern lebten, auch bei der Herrschaft gehört wurden.
     Darüber hinaus gibt es nur sehr wenige private Liedersammlun-
gen im 16. bis 17. Jahrhundert, die Scherzlieder enthalten und
wenn, dann immer nur ein einzelnes Lied.
     Das Scherzliedmaterial dagegen befindet sich in den professi-
onellen Einsammlungshandschriften, zunächst in VEDELS VISEAR-
KIV, welches aus den drei Handschriften mit den Archivbezeich-
nungen SVANING I und SVANING II, RENTZELLS HÅNDSKRIFT
sowie aus einer vierten jetzt verlorengegangenen Handschrift, alle
etwa aus dem Jahre 1580, besteht. Es sind ferner ausschliesslich
die Aufzeichner, die von Iørn Piø in NYE VEJE TIL FOLKEVISEN 8)
ausgeschieden und mit 'menigmandsoptegnere' (Volksaufzeichner)
bezeichnet wurden, d.h. Aufzeichner, die ihren Umgang mit Bür-
gern und Bauern hatten und hier dieses realistisches Material
eingefangen haben. - Ein in dieser Hinsicht besonders guter und

7.   Rita Pedersen: Visehåndskrifter på Rosenholm. Ide Giøes vise-
     bog. Håndskrifts- og visetraditionsanalyser. Arbeitsmaterial.
8.   Iørn Piø: Nye veje til folkevisen. Studier i Danmarks gamle
     folkeviser. Kopenhagen: Gyldendal, 1985.

aktiver Aufzeichner ist der Schreiber, der SVANING II,1 9) bezeichnet wird. Dieser Schreiber hat insgesamt 26 Lieder aufgezeichnet, von denen 10 Scherzliedern (jetzt in DS herausgegeben), 5
scherzenden Liedern (etwas zufällig in DgF herausgegeben) sind,
während 8 Lieder ein historisches Thema haben. Wieder regt es
zum Nachdenken an, dass das Interesse des Einsammlers und
Schreibers, das ein historisches ist, zugleich in eine, man könnte
sagen, *gesellschaftskritische Richtung* geht durch einen Teil der
aufgezeichneten Scherzlieder. Der Historiker Anders Sørensen Vedel ist selbst nicht davor zurückgewichen, ein Paar provozierenden
Scherz- und Spottlieder aufzuzeichnen. Diese professionelle Einsammlertätigkeit, die Ende des 16. Jahrhunderts stattfand, hat uns
also ein bedeutendes, differenziertes Bild der alten Liedtradition
gegeben.

Eine neue Einsammlertätigkeit professioneller Art fand in der
ersten Hälfte des 17. Jahrhunderts statt und nun galt es hauptsäch-
lich der Flugschriftliedern - Die adlige Dame Vibeke Bild war die
Urheberin einer Sammlung von drei Liederhandschriften mit zusammen über 300 Texten. Es ist deutlich, dass in vielen Fällen von
direkten Abschriften nach Flugblättern die Rede ist, da das Titel-
blatt mit Verfasser- und Melodieangaben oft zusammen mit dem
Lied oder - falls das Flugblatt mehrere Lieder enthielt - mit den
Liedern abgeschrieben wurde.

Ein Teil dieser abgeschriebenen Scherzlieder ist heute nicht
mehr gedruckt überliefert und ist deshalb für die Forschung der
alten Flugschriftentradition wertvoll. Sie sind zugleich ein vollgül-
tiger Beweis für eine grosse, jetzt verlorene Flugschriftliederproduktion. Diese Sammlung, die vom LABORATORIUM FOR FOLKE-
SPROGLIG MIDDELALDERLITTERATUR noch nicht zu Ende be-
handelt ist, enthält ausser einer Anzahl bekannter Scherzlieder aus
dänischer und norwegischer Tradition auch deutsches Liedmaterial,
das vermutlich noch mehrere Scherzlieder älteren und neueren
Ursprungs birgt. Die Sammlung kann uns zweifellos weitere Kennt-

9.   DgF XII, Seite 321-24,
     Iørn Piø og Rita Pedersen: Dronningens Visebog. Viser indsam-
     let af en folkemindesamler i sekstende århundrede. Med tilret-
     telagte og harmoniserede melodier fortrinsvis fra nittende
     århundredes tradition. Kopenhagen: Foreningen Danske Folke-
     minder, 1984.

nisse über die Beziehung zwischen der dänischen Scherzlieder- und Flugschriftliedertradition und der norwegischen und deutschen geben.

Die beiden *professionellen Liedersammlungen* - mit einer dazwischenliegenden Zeitspanne von etwa 50 Jahren - und die *private Sammlung* in Rosenholm illustrieren, dass dort, wo die Liederhandschrift nicht länger allein ein *Poesiebuch* - wie z.b. HJERTEBOGEN und JOHANN VENSTERMANDS OG KAREN GYLDENSTJERNES VISEBOG (Archivbezeichnung: LANGEBEKS KVART) - oder eine *Liederanthologie* ist, die auf ein für Adelskreise interessantes und abgegrenztes Thema konzentriert ist - wie z.b. MARGRETHE LANGES VISESAMLING (Archivbezeichnung: KAREN BRAHES FOLIO) und in ausgeprägtem Grad die 70 Jahre jüngere KAREN CHRISTENDATTERS VISEBOG - sondern eine breitere Einsammlung, die sich über das adlige Milieu und die adligen Interessengebieten hinausbewegt, hinaus zu den schlichteren Bevölkerungsgruppen mit ihren Problemen, dort erhalten wir ganz selbstverständlich einen weitaus variierteren Eindruck von der ältesten dänischen Liedtradition als eine lebendige und alle angehende Mitteilungsform. Dort wo - um die Bezeichnung von DgF zu verwenden - 'Ridderviserne' nicht ohne weiteres die Gesellschaft, in der sie überliefert wurden, beleuchten können - und schon gar nicht die Art von Liedern, die die Handlung in einem konstruierten Mittelaltermilieu, das von stereotypen Agierenden bevölkert ist, abspielen lässt - dort lässt sich der Teil der Liedtradition, der sich mit den schlichten menschlichen Verhältnissen befasst: die scherzenden, spottenden, provozierenden, ironisierenden und parodierenden Lieder als zeiterklärende Texte auffassen und verwenden. Je schärfer, je derber sie sind, je realistischer ist vermutlich das Bild der Gesellschaft, welches sie vermitteln.

Besonders die hier genannte Liederbücher sind ergiebiges Material für den Liedforscher, aber es voraussetzt, dass wir diese Liederbücher - diese wichtige Quellen - als Ganzes, ohne Überlieferungsmaterial auszustossen - ungeteilt brauchen.

Wir haben jahraus und jahrein über verlorengegangenen Handschriften und verlorengegangenen Flugblätter geklagt. Iørn Piø hat nun in seinem Buch NYE VEJE TIL FOLKEVISEN mit Spuren verlorengegangender Quellen zu arbeiten versucht. - Diese Idee führt die Liederforschung in einer positiver Richtung. - Haben wir sehr wichtige Quellen verloren - und ich denke hier an die ältesten

Flugblätter und die älteste mündliche volkstümliche Gesangtradition - dann haben wir doch in vielen Fällen die Spuren der verlorengegangener Quellen in VEDELS VISEARKIV und in andere Handschriften zurück. Diese Spuren sind für mich sehr wichtige, wenn ich die ältesten dänischen Gesangtradition - als Ganzes - zu betrachten wünsche.

Wir müssen nicht nur die Quellen - aber auch die Spuren verlorengegangener Quellen in der eksistierender Quellen benutzen um einer Verzeichnung der Liedertradition zu entgehen.

Für den Traditionswissenschaftler und für den inhaltsanalysierenden Textwissenschaftler enthalten die genannten Sammlungen: VEDELS VISEARKIV, VIBEKE BILDS INDSAMLING sowie JENS BILLES, IDE GIØES und SOPHIA SANDBERGS VISEBØGER wie genannt ergiebiges Forschnungsmaterial.

Und dann sind wir bei diesen Sammlungen vielleicht doch um Scherz-und Spottlieder oder sonstiges gutes Material gebracht worden. In den drei erwähnten privaten Sammlungen, JENS BILLES, IDE GIØES und SOPHIA SANDBERGS VISEBØGER gibt es Lakunen. Es fehlen Blätter - und in einigen Fällen befinden sich die Lakunen gerade an den Stellen, an denen Bruchstücke von Scherzliedern vorkommen. In JENS BILLES VISEBOG gibt es eine Lakune (in der Paginierung von Svend Grundtvig:) zwischen Blatt 20 und 21, so dass wir nur Bruchstücke der Lieder über "Torkel og Ølkonen" und über "De to Søstre" erhalten (hrsg. in HGrN's DANSKE VISER 10) als DV 87 und DV 85 und bei ETKr in der Scherzlieder-Ausgabe als DSk 67 und DSk 65). - Ferner gibt es eine Lakune zwischen Blatt 60 und 61, so dass der Schluss eines Liedes über "Marsk Stig" (DgF 145E) und der Anfang eines stark provozierenden Liedes (DS 7) über "kærlingen", die von einem Hofman gekränkt wird und diesen tötet, fehlen. Sie wird nicht mit Wasser und Brot 'bestraft', sondern mit herrlichem "Flæsk" (Speck) - und selbstverständlich beharrt sie, und "hver en hofmand", der sie in Zukunft kränkt, "slår hun hårdt mod jord" (jeden Hofman.... schlägt sie hart zu Boden). Das Lied ist in der Tradition des 19. Jahrhunderts verbreitet, aber auch der erwähnte 'menigmandsoptegner' (Volksaufzeichner) in VEDELS

---

10. DV: Hakon Grüner-Nielsen: Danske Viser fra Adelsvisebøger og Flyveblade 1530-1630 I-VI, Kopenhagen: Gyldendal, 1912-31.

VISEARKIV 11) hat "Jeg haver så fri en hofmand myrd'" (=DS 7: "Kællingen til Skrifte").

In IDE GIØES VISEBOG befindet sich möglicherweise eine Lakune zwischen Blatt 32 und 33, wo auf der einen Seite ein Scherzlied (DS 13) über "Hr. Jenses Brødre og Ræven" und auf der entgegengesetzten Seite das Lied von "Den store Due" (DS 9) steht, eine Variante des in der Tradition des 19. Jahrhunderts bekannten Liedes, das nicht ganz 'wohlanständig' ist, und in dem es um die Zerteilung von "Den store Krage" geht. Dass in IDE GIØES VISE-BOG hier an einer Stelle die Bezeichnung "de bønder" (die Bauern) statt "vi bønder" (wir Bauern) verwendet wird, deutet darauf hin, dass diese Variante eine adlige Verarbeitung mit 'der Feder in der Hand' ist. Im übrigen ist die Scherzliedüberlieferung dadurch charakterisiert, dass entweder keine oder nur eine sehr behutsame Bearbeitung erfolgt ist.

In unseren übrigen Liederhandschriften gibt es hier und da Lakunen, die sich nur selten rekonstruieren lassen, da die wenigsten Handschriften über ein Inhaltsverzeichnis verfügen. - Wir wissen nicht, ob die fehlenden Blätter Scherzliedmaterial enthalten haben, das entweder von Volkskundlern aus Interesse oder aus Gründen der Anständigkeit entfernt worden ist, wenn sie etwa besonders derbe Lieder enthalten haben. - Wir wissen deshalb nicht, was von der schlichten volkstümlichen Tradition nicht aufgezeichnet ist und was nach der Aufzeichnung verlorengegangen ist.

Ausser den festgestellten Verdrängungen von Scherz- und Spottliedmaterial auf dem Mitteiler-, Aufzeichner- und Herausgeberstadium, müssen wir mit einer zusätzlichen Verzeichnung der Liedtradition rechnen, die in den Fällen entsteht, in denen es für den wissenschaftlichen Bearbeiter des Scherzliedmaterials durch die u.a. in DgF angewandte Herausgeberpraxis schwierig wird, ein in dieser Hinsicht besonders ergiebiges Material zu entdecken.

Ein einzelnes aber sehr anschauliches Beispiel:

Der mehrmals erwähnte 'menigmandsoptegner' in VEDELS VISE-ARKIV: SVANING II,1 hat ein scherzendes Lied über die beiden tapferen Helden "Helled Hagen" und "Falkvor Spillemand". 12) Dieses Lied wird seriös in DgF unter der Gruppe literarisch

---

11. Dronningens Visebog Nr. 10.
12. Dronningens Visebog Nr. 22.

inspirierter Lieder über "Grimilds Hævn" (DgF 5) herausgegeben,
wobei der Herausgeber, Svend Grundtvig, nicht nur die Strophenrei-
henfolge sondern auch die Form des SVANING-Schreibers von
acht-Linien-Strophen (die vermutlich von einem Flugblatt herrüh-
ren) ändert, und zwar zu der allmählich akzeptierten 'folkevise'-
Strophe mit vier Linien.

Dieser Beitrag führt uns nun zu einer Frage an die Kollegen: Hat
Evald Tang Kristensen recht, wenn er sagt, dass "vore nabolande",
wenn wir "forgjæves må lede efter sidestykker til flere af disse
viser" (skæmteviser) - in der gleichen Verlegenheit gewesen sind
wie er? - Direkt ausgedrückt: In welchem Ausmass ist in Schweden,
Norwegen, Deutschland und England von einer Ungenauigkeit in der
überlieferten Liedtradition wegen Verdrängungen und zufälligem
oder erwünschtem Verlust des sehr wichtigen Teils der alten
volkstümlichen Tradition, welche die scherzende Tradition dar-
stellt, die Rede? - Und hat die verwendete Herausgeberpraxis ihren
Anteil zu einer weiteren Verzeichnung der Liedtradition beigetragen? Welchen und wie gross einen Teil des gesammten überlieferten Scherzliedmaterials machen z.B. die Scherzlieder aus, die in
den zukünftigen Bänden der SVERIGES MEDELTIDA BALLADER
13) und NORSKE MELLOMALDARBALLADER 14) herausgegeben
werden?
  Meine Fragen sollen natürlich als provozierende Fragen aufge-
fasst werden, und sie können hoffentlich eine Diskussion hervorru-
fen!

Universität Odense

13. SMB: Sven-Bertil Jansson, Margareta Jersild, Bengt R. Jonsson
    u.a.: Sveriges Medeltida Ballader I-IX (im Druck und in An-
    satz), I: Naturmytiska visor, Stockholm: Svenskt Visarkiv,
    1983.
14. NMB: Ådel Gjøstein Blom, Øystein Gaukstad, Nils Schiørring
    u.a.: Norske mellomalderballader I-? (im Druck und in Ansatz),
    I: Legendeviser, Oslo-Bergen-Tromsø: Universitetsforlaget,
    1982.

Opposition von *Sven-Bertil Jansson*

Die Aufforderung, das Singen, 'the singing activities' zu studieren, ist zweifellos nicht nur berechtigt sondern sogar notwendig. Dass bei einem solchen Studium die Frage, warum gesungen wird, ins Zentrum des Interesses gerückt wird, scheint mir eine Parallele zu sein zu der in der Literaturwissenschaft schon längst aktualisierten Frage nach dem Bedürfnis, dem der Text entgegenkommt. Auch wenn wir zu den Balladen kommen, müssen wir - auch die Text-forscher - uns die Tatsache vor den Augen halten, dass diese Lider wie andere gesungen wurden. So ist es selbstverständlich, dass wir beim Herausgeben von Balladen alles aus den Quellen hervorholen müssen, was von den Sängern und dem Singen wie von der Funktion spricht. Leider wird uns dieses Bestreben nicht sehr weit führen: Es gibt nur begrenzte Möglichkeiten, 'singing activity' in älteren Zeiten zu studieren.

Nach diesen Bemerkungen anlässlich der gestrigen Diskussion werde ich Rita Pedersens Vortrag kommentieren. Dabei gehe ich von der banalen Tatsache aus, dass Texte und Melodien doch auch aus älteren Zeiten vorhanden sind. Sie sind Hervorbringungen vieler Generationen, der Tradition: das Resultat schöpferischer Rezeption.

Das wenig studierte Scherzlied wurde von Rita Pedersen mit Recht in Angriff genommen. Sie ging dabei von der Auffassung aus, dass wir ein unzulängliches Bild von der Scherzliedtradition hätten, da von dieser Liederkategorie so viel verlorengegangen wäre.

Dass die Scherzlieder nicht so systematisch gesammelt wurden wie andere Lieder, ist offenbar. Ein wichtiger Grund dazu war die moralische Abneigung von Seiten der Aufzeichner oder Sammler. Beispiele wie Rita Pedersen sie aus der Zeit von Tang Kristensen anführt, liessen sich leicht vermehren.

Gegen die Ansicht, dass die Scherzlieder wegen Verdrängungen und anderer, teilweise gewollter, Verluste, uns in ungenügendem Ausmasse bekannt seien, wäre eigentlich nicht viel einzuwenden. Mit Ausgangspunkt im schwedischen Balladenmaterial möchte ich aber versuchen, eine wenn nicht konträre so doch etwas andere Meinung zu vertreten. Dabei möchte ich zuerst einige Zahlen anführen; im folgenden werde ich mich auch an vielen alten Begriffen festhalten.

In *Danmarks gamle Folkeviser* (DgF) finden wir 539 Lieder-
typen, im entsprechenden schwedischen Material nicht mehr als
210. Die Gesamtzahl der schwedischen Balladentypen aber ist 260;
in dieser Zahl sind auch einige Typen mit eingerechnet, die nur bei
uns belegt wurden, und ausserdem die Scherzballaden. Die folgende
Tabelle zeigt die prozentuelle Verteilung der skandinavischen Balladen auf die verschiedenen Hauptgruppen ('Naturmytiska visor',
'Legendvisor', 'Historiska visor', 'Riddarvisor', 'Kämpavisor' bez.
'Skämtvisor', d.h. 'Scherzlieder', in den DgF-Zahlen sind um den
Vergleich zu ermöglichen selbstverständlich auch die Scherzballaden laut *The Types of the Scandinavian Medieval Ballad* 1) eingerechnet).

	Nat.-myt.v.	Legendv.	Hist.v.	Riddarv.	Kämpav.	Skämtv.
DgF	10%	5	5,5	66	3,5	10
NMB	17	5,5	4,5	50,5	7,5	15
SMB	14	7	4	50,5	9	15,5

2)

Wir haben natürlich keine Ahnung, wie viele Balladen verschiedener
Kategorien einmal existiert haben. Von meinem Ausgangspunkt ist
diese Statistik doch nicht uninteressant. Was hier auffällt, ist ja
nicht etwa ein besonders geringer Anteil an Scherzliedern. Im
Gegenteil, die Scherzliedergruppe ist grösser als jede andere Kate-
gorie mit Ausnahme der Riddarvisor und im NMB auch der 'Naturmytiska visor'.

Rita Pedersens Frage, ob auch bei uns in Schweden von einem
ungenauen Traditionsbild geredet werden kann, muss ich mit "Ja"
beantworten. Es stellt sich aber die Frage, was diese Tatsache zu
bedeuten habe, wenn die anderen Liederkategorien in noch geringe-
rem Ausmasse überliefert seien und nur die 'Riddarvisor' eine
erheblich grössere Anzahl darstellen? Wenn man ein besonderes

1. <u>TSB</u>: Bengt R. Jonsson, Svale Solheim, Eva Danielson: <u>The
   Types of the Scandinavian Medieval Ballad</u>, Stockholm:
   Svenskt Visarkiv, Oslo-Bergen-Tromsö: Universitetsforlaget,
   1978.
2. <u>DgF</u>, <u>SMB</u>, <u>NMB</u>: Noten 1, 13 und 14, Seite 114 und 124.

Gewicht auf das Verschwinden von Scherzliedern legen will, muss man denn nicht diese Tatsache in Zusammenhang damit sehen, was mit den anderen Kategorien geschehen ist? Wäre z.B. eine wichtige Frage nicht: Warum besteht das erhaltene Balladenmaterial aus mehr als 50 oder 60 % 'Riddarvisor'?

Da Rita Pedersen von ihrer Beschäftigung mit den Liederhandschriften der 16. und 17. Jahrhunderte ausging, werde ich ein Paar Bemerkungen zu den entsprechenden schwedischen Handschriften machen. Anhand einer oberflächlichen Untersuchung möchte ich folgendes feststellen:

1) Scherzlieder wurden nur selten in diese Handschriften eingetragen: In den 12 Handschriften sind nur 12 Scherzliedertypen vertreten.

2) Von den als Balladen klassifizierten Scherzliedern finden wir nicht mehr als 5 Typen. Aber wiederum: Von den 'Legendvisor' und den historischen Liedern sind auch nur 6 bez. 7 Typen da.

3) Nur zwei Liederhandschriften aus den 16. und 17. Jahrhunderten enthalten eine grössere Menge Balladen. Erstens: *Die Handschrift Vs 20* in der Königl. Bibl. Stockholm, eine Sammlung die von professioneller Sammlertätigkeit zeugt (darin finden wir z.B. die Aufzeichnungen nach Ingierd Gunnarsdotter, der ältesten mit Namen bekannten Liedersängerin in Schweden). Fast alle Texte (um die 60) in dieser Handschrift sind Balladen. Zweitens: *Die Handschrift von Petter Rudebeck*, dem professionellen Sammler aus Ende des 17. Jahrhunderts; darin sind 42 Liederversionen vorhanden, von denen 37 Balladen sind, darunter zwei Scherzlieder.

Zusammenfassend lässt hierzu sagen: In den Liederhandschriften der beiden Jahrhunderte ist für die Ballade wenig Platz - mit Ausnahme der zwei zuletzt erwähnten Sammlungen. Dafür überwiegen andere Gattungen. Die grosse Mehrzahl besteht aus Liebesliedern im Stil der Zeit, beliebt von den mehr oder weniger aristokratischen Besitzern und Besitzerinnen der Handschriften, und aus Liedern moralischen und geistlischen Charakters. Von den Balladen sind natürlicherweise die meisten 'Riddarvisor', wenn auch eine erhebliche Anzahl von 'Kämpavisor' da zu finden sind (beim Sammler Rudebeck sogar mehr als 'Riddarvisor').

Diese Beobachtungen führen mich zu *dem* Schluss, dass die Balladen unter den Liebhabern, die sich Handschriften leisten konnten, nicht besonders attraktiv waren (anders aber bei den professionellen Sammlern). Ähnlich verhält es sich mit den Scherz-

liedern - Balladen oder nicht. Diese Liebhaber ziehen ganz einfach
andere Gattungen vor. Hier ist also keine Unterstützung für die
These zu finden, dass die Scherzlieder in besonderem Ausmasse
verdrängt wurden.

Was hat nun dies mit dem "concept of tradition" zu tun? Es ist
jedenfalls lehrreich darüber nachzudenken, dass von den Balladen
überhaupt wenig bekannt ist. Die Versionen einer bestimmten
Ballade sind ja unendlich an Zahl - und die meisten mit dem
Augenblick als sie gesungen wurden für immer verloren. Jede hat
ihren Kontext gehabt, von dem wir nunmehr nicht viel wissen
können. Dazu gehört auch das ganze Repertoar eines bestimmten
Sängers, im historischen Material wenig bekannt. In dieser Sicht
stellt das Studium der Balladen als Gattung eine fragwürdige
Isolierung des Materials dar.

Members and associate members of the symposium

Lone Albrecht
Robin D.S. Allan
Joanna R. Allan
Flemming G. Andersen
Lise Præstgaard Andersen
Ulla Andersson
Anneli Asplund
Annelise Bach
Kirsten Sass Bak
Connie Beck
Else Bekker-Nielsen
Hans Bekker-Nielsen
Karen Bekker-Nielsen
Ådel G. Blom
Marianne Novrup Børch
David Buchan
Gunilla Byrman
Birte Carlé
Michael Chesnutt
Jákup Christiansen
Helle Degnbol
Karen Kjer Dickmeiss
Kirstin Didriksen
Marie van Dijk
Dorrit Einersen
Sigrid Engeler
Beatrice La Farge
Renate Frielitz
Andreas Haarder

Kirsten Haarder
Britt Haarløv
Jan Ragnar Hagland
Eyvind Fjeld Halvorsen
Guðrún O. Helgadóttir
Thorbjörg Helgadóttir
Michael Herslund
Dietrich Hofmann
Otto Holzapfel
Lars Huldén
Ann-Mari Häggman
Sven-Bertil Jansson
Helle Jensen
Minna Skafte Jensen
Søren Skovgaard Jensen
Judith Jesch
Thelma Jexlev
Jørgen Højgaard Jørgensen
Arnfinnur Johansen
Bengt R. Jonsson
Detlev Jordan
Jonna Kjær
Kirsten Kjærulff
Jens Henrik Koudal
Hans Krog
Reimund Kvideland
Lis Helmer Larsen
Wibke Rickers Larsen
Karin Lidell

130

Louise Lillie
John Lind
Jonna Louis-Jensen
Flemming Lundgreen-Nielsen
Ole Lund-Hansen
Julia McGrew
Marianne Merrild
Anette Mogensen
Ole Munch-Pedersen
Else Mundal
Ervin Nielsen
Hans Frede Nielsen
Lars Nielsen
Svend Nielsen
Morten Nøjgaard
Søren Noe-Nygaard
Mortan Nolsöe
Tore S. Nyberg
Vésteinn Ólason
Jens E. Olesen
Michel Olsen
Thorkil Damsgaard Olsen
Ivar Orgland
Birte Ovesen
Hermann Pálsson
Carl Th. Pedersen
Rita Pedersen

Viggo Hjørnager Pedersen
Uwe Helm Petersen
Thomas Pettitt
Iørn Piø
Alex A.A. Quaade
Hanna K. Quaade
Gunnar Ries
Christopher Sanders
Kurt Schier
Uta Schier-Oberdorffer
Reinhold Schröder
Heinrich W. Schwab
Birgitte Seider
Hubert Seelow
Anne Mygind Sørensen
Bengt Algot Sørensen
Preben Meulengracht Sørensen
Horst Steinmetz
Aage Trommer
Arnfinnur Thomassen
Gudrun Utterström
Laila Vergmann
Elisabeth Vestergaard
Torben Anders Vestergaard
Mette Wad
Erik Koed Westergaard
Mogens K. With

UNIVERSITY OF WINCHESTER
LIBRARY

Publications from The Medieval Centre

Oral Tradition – Literary Tradition. A Symposium. Edited by Hans Bekker-Nielsen, Peter Foote, Andreas Haarder, Hans Frede Nielsen. Odense, 1977. 121 pp. Dan.kr. 60.00.

The European Medieval Ballad. A Symposium. Edited by Otto Holzapfel in collaboration with Julia McGrew and Iørn Piø. Odense, 1978. 121 pp. Dan.kr. 80,00.

Hans Frede Nielsen, **De germanske sprog. Baggrund og gruppering.** Odense, 1979. 130 pp. Dan.kr. 80,00.

Medieval Narrative. A Symposium. Edited by Hans Bekker-Nielsen, Peter Foote, Andreas Haarder, Preben Meulengracht Sørensen. Odense, 1979, 137 pp. Dan.kr. 130,00.

Otto Holzapfel, **Det balladeske. Fortællemåden i den ældre episke folkevise.** Odense, 1980. 122 pp. Dan.kr. 70,00. Out of print.

Preben Meulengracht Sørensen, **Norrønt Nid. Forestillingen om den umandige mand i de islandske sagaer.** Odense, 1980. 135 pp. Dan.kr. 70,00.

Medieval Iconography and Narrative. A Symposium. Edited by Flemming G. Andersen, Esther Nyholm, Marianne Powell, Flemming Talbo Stubkjær. Odense, 1980. 214 pp. Dan.kr. 110,00.

Kjalnesinge Saga eller Sagaen om Bue Andridssøn. Oversat af Jens Peter Ægidius. Odense, 1981. 90 pp. Dan.kr. 60,00. Out of print.

Hagiography and Medieval Literature. A Symposium. Edited by Hans Bekker-Nielsen, Peter Foote, Jørgen Højgaard Jørgensen, Tore Nyberg. Odense, 1981. 169 pp. Dan.kr. 120,00.

Historien om Biskop Laurentius på Holar. Oversat af Jørgen Højgaard Jørgensen. Odense, 1982. 200 pp. Dan.kr. 80,00.

The Medieval Legacy. A Symposium. Edited by Andreas Haarder, Iørn Piø. Reinhold Schröder, Preben Meulengracht Sørensen. Odense, 1982. 172 pp. Dan.kr. 140,00.

Preben Meulengracht Sørensen: **The Unmanly Man. Concepts of sexual defamation in early Northern society.** (The Viking Collection, Vol. I). Odense, 1983. 115 pp. Dan.kr. 110,00.

Flemming G. Andersen: **Commonplace and Creativity. The Role of Formulaic Diction in Anglo-Scottish Traditional Balladry.** (Odense University Studies from the Medieval Centre, vol. 1). Odense, 1985. 404 pp. Dan.kr. 250,00.

History and Heroic Tale. A Symposium. Edited by Tore Nyberg, Iørn Piø, Preben Meulengracht Sørensen, Aage Trommer. Odense, 1985. 241 pp. Dan.kr. 160,00.

The Concept of Tradition in Ballad Research. A Symposium. Edited by Rita Pedersen, Flemming G. Andersen. Odense, 1985. 132 pp. Dan.kr. 120,00.

Orders can be made through any international bookseller or direct from the publishers at the address mentioned below.

The prices are exclusive of the Danish sales tax (moms) which for the present amounts to 22 %. This sales tax is levied only in Denmark.

 Odense University Press
Odense Universitetsforlag
Pjentedamsgade 36, DK-5000 Odense C, Denmark
Telephone (09) 14 16 11 (8.30-12.00 a.m.)